WHAT MIND CONTROL
HAS DONE FOR OTHERS...

—A marketing company used it and created 18 new products.

—14 Chicago White Sox players used it and boosted their scores.

—Performing artists Vicki Carr, Carol Lawrence, and Loretta Swit have spoken about what Mind Control has done for them.

—Colleges and universities have used it to help students study less but learn more.

... MIND CONTROL
CAN DO FOR YOU!

"When persons learn to function mentally at this deeper level, creativity is enhanced. Memory is improved and persons are better able to solve problems."

> —Clancy D. McKenzie, M.D., Director,
> Philadelphia Psychiatric Consulting Service

"Highly recommended."

> —*Spiritual Studies Center Newsletter*

THE SILVA MIND CONTROL METHOD

JOSÉ SILVA
AND PHILIP MIELE

PUBLISHED BY POCKET BOOKS NEW YORK

POCKET BOOKS, a division of Simon & Schuster, Inc.
1230 Avenue of the Americas, New York, N.Y. 10020

Copyright © 1977 by José Silva

Published by arrangement with Simon and Schuster
Library of Congress Catalog Card Number: 77-1050

ISBN: 0-671-62610-8

First Pocket Books printing July, 1978

22   21   20   19   18   17   16   15   14   13

POCKET and colophon are registered trademarks
of Simon & Schuster, Inc.

Printed in the U.S.A.

ACKNOWLEDGMENTS

The authors have benefited from the wise and generous help of more friends, associates, and disinterested critics than they can ever hope to acknowledge fully. A few of them are: Marcelino Alcala, Ruth Aley, Manuel Lujan Anton, Dr. Stephen Applebaum, Robert Barnes, M.D., Joahanne Blodgett, Larry Blyden, Dr. Fred J. Bremner, Maria Luisa Bruque, Vicki Carr, Dr. Philip Chancellor, Dr. Jeffrey Chang, Dr. Erwin Di Cyan, Dr. George De Sau, Alfredo Duarte, Stanley Feller, M.D., Dord Fitz, Richard Floyd, Paul Fansella, Fermin de la Garza, Ray Glau, Pat Golbitz, Alexandro Gonzales, Reynaldo Gonzales, Father Albert Gorayeb, Ronald Gorayeb, Paul Grivas, Sister Michele Guerin, Blaz Gutierrez, Emilio Guzman, Dr. J. Wilfred Hahn, Timothy Harvey, James Hearn, Richard Herro, Larry Hildore, Celeste Holm, Joanne Howell, Margaret Huddleston, Adele Hull, Chris Jensen, Umberto Juarez, Carol Lawrence, Fred Levin, Kate Lombardi, Dorothy Longoria, Alice and Harry McKnight, Dick Mazza, Clancy D. McKenzie, M.D., Dr. James Motiff, Jose Moubayed, Jim Needham, Wingate Paine, Marguerite Piazza, Eduardo Moniz Resende, Rosa Argentina Rivas, Jose Romero, Alberto Sanchez Vilchis, M.D., Gerald Seadey, Nelda Sheets, Alexis Smith, Loretta Swit, Pat Teague, Dr. Andre Weitzenhoffer, Dr. N. E. West, Jim Williams, Lance S. Wright, M.D.

DEDICATION

To my wife, Paula, my sister, Josefina, my brother, Juan, and all my sons and daughters: José Silva, Jr., Isabel Silva de Las Fuentes, Ricardo Silva, Margarita Silva Cantu, Tony Silva, Ana Maria Silva Martinez, Hilda Silva Gonzalez, Laura Silva Lares, Delia Silva and Diana Silva.

JOSÉ SILVA

To Marjorie Miele and Grace and Bill Owen.

PHILIP MIELE

CONTENTS

INTRODUCTION

You are now setting out on one of the most transforming adventures of your life. Each result you achieve will change your view of yourself and of the world you were born into. With your new powers will come a responsibility to use them "for the betterment of mankind"— a Mind Control phrase. You cannot use them otherwise, as you are about to learn.

The city planner of a Western city closed his office door, leaving his secretary alone and troubled at her desk. The drawings for a proposed shopping mall were missing, and a yes-or-no meeting with city officials was scheduled for later that same week. Jobs have been lost for less, but the planner seemed almost untouched by what would have driven other bosses into a secretary-shattering storm.

He sat at his desk. In a moment his eyes closed and he became still and quiet. Anyone might have thought he was composing himself in the face of disaster.

A full ten minutes later he opened his eyes, rose slowly, and walked outside to his secretary. "I think I've found them," he said calmly. "Let's look at my expense account for last Thursday, when I was in Hartford. What restaurant did I have dinner in?"

He telephoned the restaurant. The drawings were there.

The city planner had been trained in Silva Mind Control, to awaken what for most of us are unused talents of the mind. One of the things he learned was to retrieve memories that have been squirreled away where the untrained mind cannot find them.

These awakened talents are doing amazing things for the more than 500,000 men and women who have taken the course.

What exactly was the city planner doing when he sat quietly for ten minutes? A report from another Mind Control graduate provides a hint:

"I had an incredible experience yesterday in Bermuda. I had two hours to get on the plane back to New York and couldn't find my plane ticket anywhere. For almost an hour, three of us searched the apartment where I'd been staying. We looked under carpets, behind the refrigerator—everywhere. I even unpacked and packed my suitcase three times, but no ticket was found. Finally I decided to find myself a quiet corner and enter my level. No sooner was I at my level than I could 'see' my plane ticket as clearly as if I were actually looking at it. It was (according to my 'level' sight) in the bottom of a closet tucked in between some books, hardly noticeable. I rushed to the closet and there was the ticket, just as I had imagined it!"

To those not trained in Mind Control, this sounds incredible, but when you come to the chapters by José Silva, Mind Control's founder, you will learn of even more amazing powers of your own mind. Perhaps most amazing of all is how easily and quickly you can learn.

Mr. Silva has devoted most of his adult life to research into what our minds can be trained to do. The result is a 40-to-48-hour course that can train anyone to remember what appears to be forgotten, to control pain, to speed healing, to abandon unwanted habits, to spark intuition so that the sixth sense becomes a creative, problem-solving part of daily life. With all this comes a cheerful inner peace, a quiet optimism based on first-hand evidence that we are more in control of our lives than we ever imagined.

Now for the first time through the printed word you can learn to practice much of what is taught in the course.

Mr. Silva has borrowed freely from both Eastern and Western learning, but the end product is quintessentially American. The course, like its founder, is totally practical. Everything he teaches is designed to help you live more happily, more effectively, here and now.

As you proceed from one exercise to another in the chapters by Mr. Silva, you will pile one success on top of another and so strengthen your confidence in yourself that you will be ready for achievements which, assuming you are not acquainted with Mind Control, you now regard as impossible. But there is scientific proof that your mind is capable of miracles. In addition, there is the successful experience of more than a half-million people whose lives Mind Control has changed.

Imagine using your mind to improve your eyesight. "While taking my first course in Silva Mind Control Method, I began to notice that my eyes were changing —seemed stronger. Prior to this I'd worn glasses ten years through childhood (till I graduated), then again started when I was thirty-eight. Always my left eye was said to be three times the weaker of the two.

"My first glasses in 1945 were reading glasses, but in '48 or '49 I began wearing bifocals—correcting always to stronger. After the course I found that, while I could not read without glasses, my eyes were certainly stronger. Since they were changing so fast, I waited as long as possible before having them checked. I even reverted to twenty-year-old glasses.

"When the local optometrist tested my eyes, he agreed that the old pair would do much better until the new lenses came."

This may seem mysterious to you now, but when you read Chapter 10 you will see exactly how graduates put their minds in charge of their bodies to speed up natural healing. The techniques are amazingly simple, as you will see in the following letter from a woman who lost 26 unwanted pounds in four months:

"First I visualized a dark frame and saw a table loaded with ice cream, cake, etc.—all the things I knew put the pounds on. I drew a large red X through the table and saw myself in a mirror that made me look very wide (the kind you find in a carnival fun house). Next I visualized a scene surrounded by golden light: a table on which all the high-protein foods rested—tuna fish, eggs, lean meat. I placed a large golden check mark on this scene and saw myself in a mirror looking very tall and thin. Mentally I told myself that I craved only the foods on the protein-laden table. I also heard all my friends telling me how fantastic I looked and saw all this happening on a specific date (this was the most important step, because I set a goal for myself). And I made it! Having been a chronic dieter, I find this the only method that has worked."

This is Mind Control—going to a deep meditative level where you can train your own mind to take charge, using its own language of images reinforced with words, bringing results that become more and more amazing, with no end in sight for the person who keeps in practice.

As you can see, this is no ordinary book. It will take you in easy steps first into meditation, then into the many ways you can use meditation until, when you reach the final step, you can do routinely what most people firmly believe cannot be done.

It is a book within a book. The outside book (chapters 1 and 2 and 17 through 20), by Philip Miele, describes the almost explosive growth of Mind Control and how it has benefited many thousands of its graduates. In the inside book, Mr. Silva shares with you many of the techniques taught in Mind Control classes. Because these classes are group experiences led by skilled lecturers, their results are speedier and more spectacular than you will achieve working alone. However, if you follow Mr. Silva's directions carefully and practice the exercises, the results are virtually certain to transform your life for the better—not as speedily, but just as certainly.

There is a special way to read this book: first read it as you would any other, from beginning to end. However, during your first reading, do not begin to practice any of the exercises. Then reread chapters 3 to 14 to get an even clearer, overall picture of the roads you are about to travel. Next read Chapter 3 and practice the exercises in it—and only those exercises—for a few weeks. When you know you are ready, go on to Chapter 4, and so on.

When you reach Chapter 14 you will already be an experienced practitioner of much that Mind Control graduates have learned. To further enrich your experience, you may wish to form a small group of friends who have practiced the same exercises. Chapter 13 tells you how to do this.

CHAPTER ONE

USING MORE OF YOUR MIND IN SPECIAL WAYS

Imagine coming into direct, working contact with an all-pervading higher intelligence and learning in a moment of numinous joy that it is on your side. Imagine too that you made this contact in such simple ways that for the rest of your life you need never again feel helplessly out of touch with something you always suspected was there but could never quite reach—a helpful wisdom, a flash of insight when you need it, the feeling of a loving, powerful presence. How would it feel?

It would be a peak experience not too different— perhaps not different at all—from spiritual awe.

This is what it feels like after four days of Silva Mind Control training. So far, more than a half-million people know; they have been through it. And as they become more accustomed to using the methods that produce this feeling they settle down into a calm, self-confident use of new powers and energies, their lives richer, healthier, freer of problems.

Shortly José Silva will explain some of these methods so that you will be able to start using them yourself. First let's look in on the beginning of a Mind Control class and see what takes place.

To start off, there is an introductory lecture of about an hour and twenty minutes. The lecturer defines Mind Control and outlines the two decades of research that led to its development. Then, briefly, he describes ways the students will be able to apply what they learn in improving health, solving everyday problems, learning more easily, and deepening spiritual awareness. A twenty-minute break follows.

Over coffee the students become acquainted. They are from widely varying backgrounds. Physicians, secretaries, teachers, taxi drivers, housewives, high-school and college students, psychiatrists, religious leaders, retired people—this is a typical mix.

After the break there is another hour-and-twenty-minute session beginning with some questions and answers, then down to business with the first training exercise, which will lead to a meditative level of mind. The lecturer explains that this is a state of deep relaxation, deeper than in sleep itself but accompanied by a special kind of awareness. It is in fact an altered state of consciousness used in virtually every meditative discipline and in intensive prayer.

No drugs or biofeedback machines are used. Mind Control lecturers speak of entering this state as "going to your level," or sometimes "going into Alpha." In a thirty-minute exercise they lead the student there gently, giving instructions in plain English. In fact all of Mind Control is in plain English: no scientific jargon or Far Eastern words.

Several of the students may already have learned to meditate before coming to class, some using methods that take a few weeks to learn, others after months of determined effort. They are amazed at a simple exercise that takes only thirty minutes.

One of the first things students hear is, "You are

learning to use more of your mind and to use it in a special manner."

This is a simple sentence they hear and internalize at the outset. The full meaning of it is nothing less than stupefying. Everyone—no exceptions—everyone has a mind that can easily be trained to exercise powers that beginners openly doubt they have. Only when they actually experience these powers do they come to believe.

Another thing that students are told is, "Project yourself mentally to your ideal place of relaxation"—a pleasant, calming, remarkably vivid exercise, which both strengthens the imagination and leads to deeper relaxation.

A word about meditation: In everyday speech it means thinking things over. If you set this book aside for a moment and consider what to have for dinner tomorrow, you are meditating.

But in the various meditative disciplines the word has a more specific meaning, referring to a special level of mind. In some disciplines, reaching this level is an end in itself, clearing the mind of all conscious thought. This produces a pleasant calm and goes a long way toward relieving and preventing illnesses caused by tension, as countless studies have proved.

But this is passive meditation. Mind Control goes far beyond this. It teaches the student to use this level of mind for solving problems, little nagging ones as well as larger, burdensome ones. This is dynamic meditation; the power of it is truly spectacular.

We hear more and more about Alpha nowadays. It is one of the brain-wave patterns, a kind of electrical energy produced by the brain, and can be measured by an electroencephalograph (EEG). The rhythms of this energy are measured in cycles per second (CPS). Generally, about fourteen CPS and up are called Beta waves; about seven to fourteen are Alpha; four to seven Theta; and four and below are Delta.

When you are wide awake, doing and achieving in the workaday world, you are in Beta, or "outer consciousness," to use Mind Control terminology. When you are daydreaming, or just going to sleep but not quite there yet, or just awakening but not yet awake, you are in Alpha. Mind Control people call this "inner consciousness." When you are asleep you are in Alpha, Theta, or Delta, not just Alpha alone, as many believe. With Mind Control training you can enter the Alpha level at will and still remain fully alert.

You may wonder what it feels like to be in these different levels of mind.

Being in Beta, or wide awake, does not produce any one particular feeling. You might feel confident or fearful, busy or idle, engrossed or bored—the possibilities in Beta are endless.

In the deeper levels the possibilities are limited for most people. Life has taught them to function in Beta, not Alpha or Theta. At these deeper levels they are pretty much limited to daydreaming, the edges of sleep, or sleep itself. But with Mind Control training, useful possibilities begin to multiply with no end in sight. As Harry McKnight, Associate Director of Silva Mind Control, wrote, "The Alpha dimension has a complete set of sensing faculties, like the Beta." In other words, we can do different things in Alpha than we can do in Beta.

This is a key concept in Mind Control. Once you become acquainted with these sensing faculties and learn to use them, you will be using more of your mind in a special manner. You will actually operate psychically whenever you want to, tapping in on Higher Intelligence.

Most people seek out Mind Control as a way to

relax, to end insomnia, to find relief from headaches, or to learn to do things that cost great efforts of will, such as stopping smoking, losing weight, improving memory, studying more effectively. This is what most of them come for; they learn much, much more.

They learn that the five senses—touching, tasting, smelling, hearing, and seeing—are only a part of the senses they were born with. There are others, call them powers or senses, once known only to a gifted few and to mystics who developed them over lifetimes removed from the active world. The mission of Mind Control is to train us to awaken these powers.

What this awakening can mean was well put by *Mademoiselle*'s beauty editor, Nadine Bertin, in the March 1972 issue:

"The drug culture can have its mind-expanding pills, powders and shots. I'll take mine straight. Mind Control does expand your mind. It teaches you HOW to expand it. It is aptly named because, unlike drugs or hypnosis, *you* are in *control*. Mind expansion, self-knowledge and helping others through Mind Control are only limited by your own limitations. ANYTHING is possible. You hear about it happening to others. And suddenly, you see it happening to you."

CHAPTER TWO

MEET JOSÉ

José Silva was born August 11, 1914, in Laredo, Texas. When he was four, his father died. His mother soon remarried, and he, his older sister, and younger brother moved in with their grandmother. Two years later he became the family breadwinner, selling newspapers, shining shoes, and doing odd jobs. In the evenings he watched his sister and brother do their homework, and they helped him learn to read and write. He has never gone to school, except to teach.

José's rise from poverty began one day when he was waiting his turn in a barbershop. He reached for something to read. What he picked up was a lesson from a correspondence course on how to repair radios. José asked to borrow it, but the barber would only rent it, and *that* on condition that José complete the examinations in the back in the barber's name. Each week José paid a dollar, read the lesson, and completed the examination.

Soon a diploma hung in the barbershop, while across town José, at the age of fifteen, began to repair radios. As the years passed, his repair business became one of the largest in the area, providing money for the education of his brother and sister, the wherewithal for him to marry, plus eventually some half-million dollars to finance the twenty years of research that led to Mind Control.

Another man with diplomas, these more conscientiously earned than the barber's, inadvertently sparked this research. The man was a psychiatrist whose job it was to ask questions of men being inducted into the Signal Corps during World War II.

"Do you wet your bed?" José was dumbfounded.

"Do you like women?" José, the father of three, and destined one day to be the father of ten, was appalled.

Surely, he thought, the man knew more about the human mind than the barber knew about radios. Why such stupid questions?

It was this perplexing moment that started José on an odyssey of scientific research that led to his becoming—without diplomas or certificates—one of the most creative scholars of his age. Through their writings, Freud, Jung, and Adler became his early teachers.

The stupid questions took on deeper meanings, and soon José was ready to ask a question of his own: Is it possible, using hypnosis, to improve a person's learning ability—in fact, raise his I.Q.? In those days I.Q. was believed to be something we were born with, but José was not so sure.

The question had to wait while he studied advanced electronics to become an instructor in the Signal Corps. When he was discharged, with savings gone and $200 in his pocket, he began slowly to rebuild his business. At the same time he took a half-time teaching job at Laredo Junior College, where he supervised three other teachers and was charged with creating the school's electronics laboratories.

Five years later, with television on the scene, his repair business began to flourish and José called a halt to his teaching career. His business once again became the largest in town. His workdays ended about nine each night. He would have dinner, help put the children to bed, and when the house was quiet, study for about three hours. His studies led him further into hypnosis.

What he learned about hypnosis, plus what he knew about electronics, plus some F's on his children's report cards brought him back to the question he had raised earlier—can learning ability, the I.Q., be improved through some kind of mental training?

José already knew that the mind generates electricity —he had read about experiments that revealed the Alpha rhythm early in this century. And he knew from his work in electronics that the ideal circuit is the one with the least resistance, or impedance, because it makes the greatest use of its electrical energy. Would the brain work more effectively too if its impedance were lowered? And *can* its impedance be lowered?

José began using hypnosis to quiet the minds of his children and he discovered what to many appeared to be a paradox: He found that the brain was more energetic when it was less active. At lower frequencies the brain received and stored more information. The crucial problem was to keep the mind alert at these frequencies, which are associated more with daydreaming and sleep than with practical activity.

Hypnosis permitted the receptivity José was looking for, but not the kind of independent thought that leads to reasoning things out so they can be understood. Having a head full of remembered facts is not enough; insight and understanding are necessary, too.

José soon abandoned hypnosis and began experimenting with mental training exercises to quiet the brain yet keep it more independently alert than in hypnosis. This, he reasoned, would lead to improved memory combined with understanding and hence to higher I.Q. scores.

The exercises from which Mind Control evolved

called for relaxed concentration and vivid mental visualization as ways of reaching lower levels. Once reached, these levels proved more effective than Beta in learning. The proof was in his children's sharply improved grades over a three-year period while he continued to improve his techniques.

José had now scored a first—a very significant one, which other research, principally biofeedback, has since confirmed. He was the first person to prove that we can learn to function with awareness at the Alpha and Theta frequencies of the brain.

Another first, an equally astonishing one, was soon to come.

One evening José's daughter had gone to her "level" (to use today's Mind Control terminology), and José was questioning her about her studies. As she answered each question, he framed the next in his mind. This was the usual procedure, and so far the session was no different from hundreds that had gone before. Suddenly, quietly, the routine was momentously changed. She answered a question her father had not yet asked. Then another. And another. She was reading his mind!

This was in 1953, when ESP was becoming a respectable subject for scientific inquiry, largely through the published work of Dr. J. B. Rhine of Duke University. José wrote to Dr. Rhine to report that he had trained his daughter to practice ESP and received a disappointing answer. Dr. Rhine hinted that the girl might have been psychic to begin with. Without tests of the girl before the training, there was no way to tell.

Meanwhile, José's neighbors noticed that his children's schoolwork had remarkably improved. At the beginning of his experiments they had been wary of his probings into the unknown, an unknown perhaps protected by forces that were best not tampered with. However, the successes of a man working with his own children could not be ignored. Would José train their children too?

After the letter from Dr. Rhine, this was just what José needed. If what he had accomplished with one child could be accomplished with others, he would have chalked up the kind of repeatable experiments that are basic to the scientific method.

Over the next ten years he trained 39 Laredo children, with even better results because he improved his techniques a little with each child. Thus another first was scored: He had developed the first method in history that can train anyone to use ESP, and he had thirty-nine repeatable experiments to prove it. Now to perfect the method.

Within another three years, José developed the course of training which is now standard. It takes only 40 to 48 hours and is as effective with adults as with children. So far it has been validated by some 500,000 "experiments," a measure of repeatability that no open-minded scientist can ignore.

These long years of research were financed by José's growing electronics business. No university or foundation or government grants were available for so far-out a field of research. Today the Mind Control organization is a thriving family business, with its profits going largely to more research and to support its accelerating growth. There are Mind Control lecturers or centers in all fifty states and in thirty-four foreign nations.

With all this success, José has not become a celebrity, nor a guru or spiritual leader with followers or disciples. He is a plain man of simple ways, who speaks with the soft, almost lost accent of a Mexican-American. He is a powerfully built, stocky man with a kindly face that creases easily into a smile.

Anyone who asks José what success has meant to

him will be answered with a flood of success stories. A few examples:

A woman wrote to the Boston *Herald American* begging for some way to help her husband, who was tormented by migraine headaches. The newspaper printed her letter, then another letter the next day from someone else, also pleading for a way to control such headaches.

A physician read these letters and wrote that she had had migraine headaches all her life. She had taken Mind Control and had not had one since. "And would you believe it, the next introductory lecture was mobbed. Absolutely mobbed."

Another physician, a prominent psychiatrist, advises all his patients to take Mind Control because it gives them insights that in some cases would require two years of therapy to produce.

An entire marketing company was organized as a co-op by graduates who used what they learned in Mind Control to invent new products and devise ways of marketing them. In its third year, the company has eighteen products on the market.

An advertising man used to need about two months to create a campaign for new clients—about average in his field. Now, with Mind Control, the basic ideas come in twenty minutes and the rest of the work is done in two weeks.

Fourteen Chicago White Sox players took Mind Control. All their individual averages improved, most of them dramatically.

The husband of an overweight woman suggested she try Mind Control because all her diets had failed. She agreed, provided he went too. She lost twenty pounds in six weeks; he stopped smoking.

A professor at a college of pharmacy teaches Mind Control techniques to his students. "Their grades are going up in all their courses, with less studying, and they're more relaxed. . . . Everybody already knows how to use his or her imagination. I just get my students to practice it more. I show them that imagination is valid and that there's a form of reality in imagination that they can use."

Although José smiles easily, when he hears "José, you've changed my life!" the smile fades a little and he says, "No, I didn't do it. *You* did, your own mind."

Now, beginning with the next chapter, José himself will show you how to use your mind to change your life.

CHAPTER THREE

HOW TO MEDITATE

*(Note: This chapter and others through Chapter 16,
by José Silva, may very well be among the most important
you have ever read. José will be teaching you
the basic elements of his Silva Mind Control course.
To benefit fully from José's chapters, be sure you have
well in mind the way to read them. You will find this
in the Introduction.)*

I am going to help you learn to meditate. When you
learn to do this, you will be at a level of mind where
you will be able to free your imagination for solving
problems. But for now we will be concerned only with
meditation; problem solving will come later on.

Because you will be learning without an experienced
guide, I will use a method slightly different and quite a
bit slower than the one we use in Mind Control classes.
You will have no trouble with it.

If you only learn to meditate and stop there, you
will be solving problems anyway. Something beautiful
happens in meditation, and the beauty you find is calming.
The more you meditate, the deeper you go within
yourself, the firmer the grasp you will have of a kind of
inner peace so strong that nothing in life will be able
to shatter it.

Your body will benefit, too. At first you will find that

29

worries and guilt feelings are absent while you are meditating. One of the beauties of meditation at the Alpha level is that you *cannot* bring your feelings of guilt and anger with you. If these feelings intrude you will simply pop out of the meditative level. As time goes on, they will stay away longer, until one day they are gone for good. This means that those activities of the mind that make our bodies sick will be neutralized. The body is designed to be healthy. It has its own healing mechanisms built in. These mechanisms are blocked by minds not trained to control themselves. Meditation is the first step in Mind Control; by itself it will go a long way toward setting free the body's healing powers and giving it back the energy once squandered on tension.*

Here is all you have to do to reach the Alpha, or meditative, level of mind:

When you awaken in the morning, go to the bathroom if necessary, then return to bed. Set your alarm for fifteen minutes later in case you drift off to sleep during the exercise. Close your eyes and look upward, behind your eyelids, at a 20-degree angle. For reasons not fully understood, this position of the eyes alone will trigger the brain to produce Alpha.

Now, slowly, at about two-second intervals, count backward from one hundred to one. As you do this, keep your mind on it, and you will be in Alpha the very first time.

In Mind Control classes students show a variety of reactions to their first experience, from "That was beautiful!" to "I didn't feel a thing." The difference is less in what happened to them than in how familiar they were with this level of mind in the first place. It will be more or less familiar to everyone. The reason for this

---

* You'll be reading about cases of this in later chapters.

is that when we awaken in the morning we are often in Alpha for a while. To go from Theta, the sleep level, to Beta, the awake level, we must pass through Alpha, and often we linger there through our early-morning routine.

If you feel that nothing happened during this first exercise, it simply means you have been in Alpha many times before without being particularly aware of it. Simply relax, don't question it, and stay with the exercises.

Even though you will be in Alpha on the very first try if you concentrate, you still need seven weeks of practice to go to lower levels of Alpha, then to Theta. Use the hundred-to-one method for ten mornings. Then count only from fifty to one, twenty-five to one, then ten to one, and finally five to one, ten mornings each.

Beginning with the very first time you go to your Alpha level, use only one method to come out of it. This will give you a greater degree of control against coming out spontaneously.

The method we use in Mind Control is to say mentally, *"I will slowly come out as I count from one to five, feeling wide awake and better than before. One— two—prepare to open your eyes—three—open eyes —four—five—eyes open, wide awake, feeling better than before."*

You will establish two routines, then, one for going to your level, the other for coming out of it. If you change the routine you will have to learn to use your new version just as you learned to use the first one. This is useless work.

Once you have learned to reach your level with the five-to-one method in the morning you are ready to enter your level any time of day that you choose. All you need is ten or fifteen minutes to spare. Because you will be entering your level from Beta rather than the light level of Alpha, a little extra training will be needed.

Sit in a comfortable chair or on a bed with your feet flat on the floor. Let your hands lie loosely in your lap. If you prefer, sit cross-legged, in the lotus position. Hold your head well balanced, not slumped. Now concentrate on first one part of the body, then another, to consciously relax it. Start with your left foot, then the left leg, then the right foot, and so on, until you reach the throat, the face, the eyes, and finally the scalp. You will be amazed the first time you do this at how tense your body was.

Now pick a spot about 45 degrees above eye level on the ceiling or the wall opposite you. Gaze at this spot until your eyelids begin to feel a little heavy and let them close. Start your countdown from fifty to one. Do this for ten days, then ten to one for another ten days, then five to one from then on. Since you will no longer be limited to the mornings for this practice, establish a routine of meditating two or three times a day, about fifteen minutes a session.

Once you reach your level, what then? What do you think about?

Right from the beginning, from the very first moment you reach your meditative level, practice visualization. This is central to Mind Control. The better you learn to visualize, the more powerful will be your experience with Mind Control.

The first step is to create a tool for visualization, a mental screen. It should be like a large movie screen but should not quite fill your mental vision. Imagine it not behind your eyelids but about six feet in front of you. You will project onto this screen whatever you choose to concentrate on. Later there will be other uses for it.

Once you have built this screen in your mind, project onto it something familiar and simple, like an orange or an apple. Each time you go to your level, stay with just one image; you may change it the next time. Concentrate on making it more and more real—in three dimensions, in full color, in all its details. Think of nothing else.

It has been said that the brain is like a drunken monkey; it lurches willy-nilly from one thing to another. It is surprising how little command we have over this brain of ours, despite the fine work it sometimes does for us. At other times, though, it operates behind our backs, treacherously creating a headache, then a rash, then an ulcer to top things off. This brain is too powerful, far too powerful, to leave out of control. Once we learn to use our minds to train it, it will do some astounding things for us, as you will soon see.

In the meantime, be patient with this simple exercise. Using your mind, train your brain to go quietly into Alpha and to attend exclusively to the job of creating a simple image more and more vividly. In the beginning, as thoughts intrude, be gently forgiving. Slowly push them away and return to the single object at hand. Becoming irritated or tense will bring you right out of Alpha.

This, then, is meditation as it is widely practiced throughout the world. If you do this and nothing else, you will experience what William Wordsworth called "A happy stillness of mind," and more, a deep and durable inner peace. This will come as an exciting experience as you reach deeper levels of mind; then you will take it more and more for granted and the excitement will pass. When this happens, many drop out. They forget that this is not a "trip" for its own sake but the first step in what may well be the most important journey they have ever taken.

CHAPTER FOUR

DYNAMIC MEDITATION

The passive meditation you have just read about (and I hope are about to experience) can be accomplished in other ways. Instead of concentrating on a visual image, you can concentrate on a sound, such as OM or ONE or AMEN, uttered aloud or mentally, or the feeling of your breathing. You can focus on an energy point of the body or on the beat of drums and dance, or you can listen to a sonorous Gregorian chant while you gaze at the familiar enactment of a religious ritual. All of these methods and some combinations of them will bring you to a calm meditative level of mind.

I prefer counting backward to get you there, because at first it takes some concentration, and concentration is the key to success. Once you have reached your level several times with this method, the method will be associated in your mind with the successful result and the process will become more automatic.

Every successful result in Mind Control becomes what we call a "reference point"—we hark back to the experience consciously or unconsciously, repeat it, and go on from there.

Once you have reached the meditative level, to simply stay there and wait for something to happen is not enough. It *is* beautiful and calming and it does contribute to your good health, but these are modest accomplishments compared with what is possible. Go beyond this passive meditation, train your mind for organized, dynamic activities—which I believe it was designed for—and the results will amaze you.

I make this point now because this is the moment for us to go beyond the passive meditation technique you have just read about and learn to use meditation dynamically to solve some problems. You will now see why the simple exercise of visualizing an apple, or whatever else you choose, on a mental screen is so important.

Now, before you go to your level, think of something pleasant—no matter how trivial—that happened yesterday or today. Review it briefly in your mind, then go well into your level and project onto your mental screen the total incident. What were the sights, the smells, the sounds, and your feelings at that time? All the details. You will be surprised at the difference between your Beta memory of the incident and your Alpha recall of it. It is almost as great as the difference between saying the word "swim" and actually swimming.

What is the value of this? First, it is a steppingstone to something bigger, and second, it is useful in itself. Here is how you can use it:

Think of something you own that is not lost but would take a little searching to find. Your car keys, perhaps. Are they on your bureau, in your pocket, in the car? If you are not sure, go to your level, think back to when you had them last, and relive that moment. Now proceed forward in time and you will locate them if they are where you left them. (If someone else took them, you have another kind of problem to solve, which requires much more advanced techniques.)

Imagine the student who remembers his instructor

saying there will be an exam this Wednesday—or did he say next Wednesday? He can settle it for himself in Alpha.

These are typical of the small, everyday problems that this simple meditational technique can solve.

Now for a giant leap forward. We are going to connect a real event with a desirable one that you imagine —and see what becomes of the imaginary one. If you operate according to some very simple laws, the imaginary event will become real.

Law 1: You must *desire* that the event take place. "The first person I see on the sidewalk tomorrow will be blowing his nose" is so useless a project to work on that your mind will turn away from it; it will probably not work. Your boss will be more agreeable, a certain customer will be more receptive to what you are selling, you will find satisfaction in a task you ordinarily find disagreeable—these are prospects that can engage a reasonable measure of desire.

Law 2: You must *believe* the event can take place. If your customer is overstocked with what you sell, you cannot reasonably believe he will be eager to buy. If you cannot believe the event can reasonably take place, your mind will be working against it.

Law 3: You must *expect* the event to take place. This is a subtle law. The first two are simple and passive—this third one introduces some dynamics. It is possible to desire an event, believe it can take place, and still not expect it to take place. You want your boss to be pleasant tomorrow, you know that he can be, but you may still be some distance from expecting it. This is where Mind Control and effective visualization come in, as we will see in a moment.

Law 4: You *cannot create* a problem. Not *may* not

but *cannot*. This is a basic, all-controlling law. "Wouldn't it be great if I could get my boss to make such an ass of himself that he'll be fired and I'll get his job?" When you are working dynamically in Alpha you are in touch with Higher Intelligence, and from the perspective of Higher Intelligence it would not be great at all. You may trip up your boss and get him fired, but you will be entirely on your own—and in Beta. In Alpha it simply will not work.

If, at your meditative level, you try to tune in to some kind of intelligence that will assist in an evil design, it will be as fruitless as trying to tune a radio to a station that does not exist.

Some accuse me of being a pollyanna on this point. Thousands of people have smiled indulgently as I spoke of the utter impossibility of doing harm in Alpha, until they learned for themselves. There is plenty of evil on this planet, and we humans perpetrate more than our share of it. This is done in Beta, not Alpha, not Theta, and probably not in Delta. My research has proved this.

I never recommend wasting time, but if you must prove this for yourself, go to your level and try to give someone a headache. If you visualize this "event" as vividly as necessary to accomplish anything at all, one or both of the following will result: You, not your intended victim, will get the headache and/or you will snap out of Alpha.

This does not answer all the questions you may have about the good and evil potentials of the mind. There will be more to say later. For the moment, choose an event that is a solution to a problem, that you desire, believe can come about, and, with the following exercise, will learn to expect.

Here is what to do:

Choose a real problem that you face, one that has not yet resolved itself. As an illustration, let us say that your boss has been ill-tempered lately. There are three steps to go through once you reach your level:

Step 1: On your mental screen, thoroughly re-create a recent event which involved the problem. Relive it for a moment.

Step 2: Gently push this scene off the screen to the *right.* Slide onto the screen another scene that will take place tomorrow. In this scene everyone around the boss is cheerful and the boss is on the receiving end of good news. He is clearly in a better mood now. If you know specifically what was causing the problem, visualize the solution at work. Visualize it as vividly as you did the problem.

Step 3: Now push this scene off the screen to the right and replace it with another from the left. The boss is happy now, fully as pleasant as you know he can be. Experience this scene as vividly as if it had actually happened. Stay with it for a while, get the full feel of it.

Now, at the count of five you will be wide awake feeling better than before. You can be confident that you have just put forces to work for you in the direction of creating the event you want.

Will this work always, invariably, without a hitch? No.

However, here is what you will experience if you keep at it: One of your very earliest problem-solving meditation sessions will work. When it does, who can say it was not a coincidence? After all, the event you chose had to be probable enough for you to believe it could materialize. Then it will work a second time, and a third. The "coincidences" will pile up. Abandon your Mind Control activities and there will be fewer coincidences. Go back to it and the coincidences multiply again.

Further, as you gradually increase your skill you will notice that you will be able to believe and expect events that are less and less probable. In time, with practice, the results you achieve will be more and more astounding.

As you work on each problem, begin by briefly reliving your best previous successful experience. When an even better successful experience comes along, drop the earlier one and use the better one as your reference point. This way you will become "better and better," to use a phrase with an especially rich meaning for all of us in Mind Control.

Tim Masters, a college student–taxi driver in Fort Lee, New Jersey, uses his waiting time between fares for meditation. When local business is slow, he puts a solution on his mental screen—someone carrying suitcases who wants to go to Kennedy Airport. "First few times I tried it . . . nothing. Then it happened—a man with suitcases going to Kennedy. Next time, I put this man on my screen, got that feeling you get when things are working, and along came another one for Kennedy. It works! It's like a winning streak that won't quit!"

Before we move on to other exercises and techniques, let me take note of something you probably wonder about: Why do we move scenes from left to right on our mental screens? I can take note of the question here but it will be dealt with in more detail later.

My experiments have shown that the deeper levels of our minds experience time flowing from left to right. In other words, the future is perceived as being on our left, the past on our right. It is tempting to go into this now, but there are other things to do beforehand.

CHAPTER FIVE

IMPROVING MEMORY

The memory techniques taught in Mind Control can reduce our use of telephone directories and tremendously impress our friends. But if I want a telephone number, I look it up. Perhaps some Mind Control graduates do use their skills for remembering telephone numbers but, as I said in the previous chapter, desire is important in making things work, and my desire to remember phone numbers is something less than spirited. If I had to cross town every time I needed a telephone number, my desire would perk up.

It is basically unsound to use Mind Control techniques for anything but important matters because of that desire, belief, expectancy trilogy. But how many of us have memories as efficient as we would like? Yours may already be improving in unexpected ways if you have mastered the techniques described in the previous two chapters. Your new ability to visualize and re-create past events while you are in Alpha has a certain carry-over to Beta, so without any special effort your mind may be working in new ways for you. Still, there is room for improvement.

In Mind Control classes we have a special visualization exercise. In this exercise the lecturer writes numbers from one to thirty on a blackboard, then the students call out the names of objects—snowball, roller skate, ear plug—whatever comes to mind. He writes each word opposite a number, turns away from the blackboard, and recites them in order. Students call out any word and the lecturer gives the corresponding number.

This is not a parlor trick but a lesson in visualization. The lecturer has already memorized a word for each number; thus each number evokes a visual image of its corresponding word. We call these images "memory pegs." When a student calls out a word, the lecturer combines it in some meaningful or fanciful way with the image he has associated with the word's number. The memory peg for ten is "toes"; if a student offers "snowball" as the tenth word, the resulting image may be a snowball on your toes. This is not difficult for a mind trained in visualization.

The students begin to learn the Memory Pegs by being at their level while the lecturer slowly repeats them. Then, when they later undertake to memorize them in Beta, the job is easier because the words seem familiar.

I must omit the Memory Pegs from this book because too much time and space would be needed here to learn them. You already have a powerful technique for improving your visualization and your memory at the same time: the mental screen.

Anything you believe you have forgotten is associated with an event. If it is a name, the event is the time you heard or read it. All that you have to do, once you learn to work with your mental screen, is visualize a past event that surrounds an incident you believe you have forgotten, and it will be there.

I say an incident you *believe* you have forgotten because in reality you have not forgotten it at all. You simply do not recall it. There is a significant difference.

The world of advertising offers us a familiar illustration of the difference between memory and recall. We all see television commercials. There are so many of them and they are so brief that if we were asked to list five or ten that we saw during the past week we would be able to cite only three or four at the most.

A major way in which advertising creates sales is by causing us to "remember" a product below the level of awareness.

It is doubtful that we ever really forget anything. Our brain squirrels away images of the most trivial events. The more vivid the image and the more important it is to us, the more easily we recall it.

An electrode gently touching an exposed brain during surgery will trigger a long-"forgotten" event in all its details, so vividly that the sounds and smells and sights are actually experienced. This, of course, is the brain being touched, not the mind. As real as the flashbacks that the brain offers up to the patient's awareness may be, he will know—something tells him—that he was not really reliving them. This is the mind at work—the super-observer, the interpreter—and no electrode has ever touched it. The mind, unlike the tip of our nose, does not exist in a specific place.

To return to memory. Somewhere thousands of miles from where you are sitting, a leaf is falling from a tree. You will not remember or recall this event because you did not experience it, nor is it important to you. However, our brains record far more events than we realize.

As you sit reading this book you are going through thousands of experiences of which you are not aware. To the extent that you are concentrating now, you are unaware of them. There are sounds and odors, sights in the corner of your eye, perhaps the small discomfort of a shoe that is too tight, the feel of your chair, the temperature of the room—there seems to be no end. We are conscious of these sensations but not aware of being conscious of them, which seems like a contradiction until we consider the case of a woman under general anesthesia.

During the course of her pregnancy, this woman had developed an excellent rapport with her obstetrician. Between the two there was friendship and confidence. Came time for her delivery and she went routinely under general anesthesia and gave birth to a healthy baby. Later, when her physician visited her in her hospital room, she was strangely distant, even hostile toward him. Neither she nor her physician could account for her changed attitude, and both were eager to find some explanation for it. They decided to try, through hypnosis, to uncover some hidden memory that might explain her sudden change.

Under hypnosis she was led through time regression, from her most recent experience with her physician back to earlier ones. They did not have far to go. In a deep trance, instead of skipping over the period when she was "unconscious" in the delivery room, she recounted everything the doctor and nurses had said. What they said in the presence of the anesthetized patient was at times clinically detached, at other times humorous, and at other times they expressed annoyance at the slow progress of her delivery. She was a thing, not a person; her feelings were not considered. After all, she was unconscious, wasn't she?

I question whether it is possible ever to be unconscious. We either can or cannot recall what we experience, but we are always experiencing and all experiences leave memories firmly printed on the brain.

Does this mean that with the memory techniques you

are about to learn you will be able ten years from now to recall the number of this page? You may not have looked at it, but it is there; you saw it out of the corner of your eye, so to speak. Perhaps, but probably not. It is not and probably never will be important to you.

But can you recall the name of that attractive person you met at dinner last week? When you first heard the name, the hearing of it was an event. You need simply re-create the surrounding event on your Mental Screen, as I have explained, and you will hear the name again. Relax, go to your level, create the screen, experience the event. This takes fifteen or twenty minutes. But we have another way, a sort of emergency method, which will take you instantly to a level of mind where recall of information will be easier.

This method involves a simple triggering mechanism which, once it becomes really yours, improves in effectiveness as you use it. Making it yours will require several meditation sessions to thoroughly internalize the procedure. Here is how simple it is: Just bring together the thumb and first two fingers of either hand and your mind will instantly adjust to a deeper level. Try it now and nothing will happen; it is not yet a triggering mechanism. To make it one, go to your level and say to yourself (silently or aloud), "Whenever I join my fingers together like this"—now join them—"for a serious purpose I will instantly reach this level of mind to accomplish whatever I desire."

Do this daily for about a week, always using the same words. Soon there will be a firm association in your mind between joining the thumb and two fingers and instantly reaching an effective meditation level. Then, one day soon, you will try to recall something— someone's name, for example—and the name will not come. Try harder and it will even more stubbornly refuse to come. The will is not only useless; it is a hindrance. Now relax. Realize that you remember and that you have a way of triggering recall.

A teacher of fourth-graders in Denver uses the Mental Screen and the Three Fingers Technique to teach spelling. She covers about twenty words a week. To test them, instead of going from one word to another and asking for the correct spelling, she asks the students to write down all the words they studied that week. They remember the words *and* how to spell them —with their three fingers together, seeing them on their mental screens. "The slower ones," she says, "take about fifteen minutes with the test."

Using the same technique, she teaches these fourth-graders the multiplication table up to the 12's by November; this normally takes an entire school year.

Tim Masters, the college student–taxi driver mentioned in the last chapter, often gets passengers who want to go to addresses in neighboring towns where he has been so long ago that his memory of how to get there has dimmed. Not many hurried passengers would understand if he went into meditation before starting off. But with his three fingers together, he "relives" the last time he drove there.

Before he took Mind Control, Tim's grades at New York Institute of Technology were all B's and one A. "Now I'm a scholar—all A's and one B," he reports. He uses Speed Learning when he studies—you will read about this in the next chapter—and he takes exams with his three fingers together.

There are other uses for this Three Fingers Technique, which you will read about later. We use it in several unusual ways. It has been associated with other meditative disciplines for centuries. The next time you see a painting or sculpture of a Far Eastern person—a Yogi, perhaps, sitting cross-legged in meditation—notice that the three fingers of his hands are similarly joined.

CHAPTER SIX

SPEED LEARNING

When you learn the memory techniques in the last chapter you will be well on your way to our next step, Speed Learning. Briefly, this is how you will progress: You will learn to enter the meditative level; then, at that level, to create a mental screen, which is useful for various purposes, one of which is to recall information. Then, as a shortcut, you will learn the Three Fingers Technique for, among other things, instant recall. Once you have accomplished this you will be ready for new ways of acquiring information, making recall even easier. Equally important, these new ways of learning will not only make recall easier but will both speed up and deepen your understanding of what you learn.

There are two learning techniques. Let's start with the simpler, though not necessarily the easier, one.

The Three Fingers Technique, once it is so thoroughly mastered that you can instantly reach your level and operate consciously there, can be used while you listen to a lecture or read a book. This will vastly improve concentration, and information will be implanted more firmly. Later you will be able to recall it more easily at the Beta level and more easily still at the Alpha level. A student writing an exam with his three fingers together

46

can almost see the textbook he read, almost hear the instructor as he discussed the lesson in class.

The other technique is not as simple, but you will be ready for it earlier in your practice of Mind Control. It has all the effectiveness of learning at the Alpha level plus the added reinforcement of learning at Beta. You will need a tape recorder for this.

Let us say that you have a complex chapter of a textbook to learn; you must not only remember but understand it. During the first step, do not go into Alpha but remain at outer consciousness, Beta. Read the chapter aloud into the recorder. Now go to your level, play it back, and concentrate on your own voice as it recites the material.

At an early stage of your Mind Control, particularly if you are not too familiar with the machine you are using, you may flip back to Beta when you push the playback button and find that the sound of the tape will make it more difficult to return to Alpha. By the time you do return, you will have missed part or all of the lesson. With practice, this is less likely to happen. Here are a few tips:

Go to your level with your finger already on the button. This will prevent your having to search for it with your eyes open.

Have someone else press the playback for you when you give the signal.

Use the Three Fingers Technique to speed up your re-entry into Alpha.

The problem may appear more serious than it is. In fact, it may actually be an indication of your progress. As you become more adept, the Alpha level itself will begin to feel different. It will feel more and more like Beta because you will be learning to use it consciously.

Being wide awake with full mental effectiveness while at Alpha is a special feature of Mind Control.

As you progress and recapture the earlier feeling of being at Alpha, you are really going to a deeper level, perhaps Theta. In Mind Control classes I have often seen graduates operating effectively at a deep level with eyes open, fully as awake as you are now, speaking clearly, asking and answering questions, cracking jokes.

Back to your tape recording: For added reinforcement, let some time pass, several days if possible, then read the material again at Beta and play it back in Alpha. The information will now be firmly yours.

If you are working with others in learning Mind Control with this book, you may exchange tapes in a sort of division of labor to save time. This works perfectly well, though there is a slight advantage to listening to your own voice.

Speed Learning and the Three Fingers Technique have proved to be valuable time-savers for Mind Control graduates in a number of fields—sales (particularly insurance), academic study, teaching, law, and acting to name just a few.

A successful Canadian life insurance agent no longer exasperates his clients by riffling through the papers in his briefcase to find answers to their questions about complex estate and tax problems. The tremendous array of facts he needs are on the tip of his tongue, thanks to Speed Learning and his three fingers.

A trial lawyer in Detroit has "liberated" himself from notes when he sums up a complex case to a jury. He records his summation and listens to it in Alpha the night before, then again early the next morning. Later, when he stands confidently before the jurors, he maintains reassuring eye contact with them. The result is that he speaks more persuasively than if he were consulting notes, and no one notices what he does with the three fingers of his left hand.

A New York night club comedian changes his routine every day; he "comments" on the news. An hour before show time he listens to a tape of himself and he is ready with twenty minutes of "spontaneous" high humor. "I used to cross my fingers, hoping for the best. Now I join three fingers and I know what's going to happen—lots of laughs."

Speed Learning and the Three Fingers Technique, of course, are ideal for students—one reason why Mind Control has so far been taught in twenty-four colleges and universities, sixteen high schools, and eight grade schools. Thanks to these techniques, thousands of students are studying less and learning more.

CHAPTER SEVEN

CREATIVE SLEEP

How free we are when we dream! The barriers of time, the limitations of space, the laws of logic, the constraints of conscience are all swept away and we are gods of our own fleeting creations. Because what we create is uniquely ours, Freud placed central importance on our dreams. Understand a man's dreams, he seemed to say, and you understand the man.

In Mind Control we take dreams seriously, too, but in a different way because we learn to use our minds in different ways. Freud dealt with dreams that we create spontaneously. Not Mind Control. Our interest is in deliberately creating dreams to solve specific problems. Because we program their subject matter beforehand, we interpret them differently—with spectacular results. Though this limits the spontaneity of our dreaming experiences, we gain a significant freedom: greater control over our lives.

When we interpret a dream which we preprogram, in addition to gaining insights into the pathology of our psyches, we find solutions to everyday problems.

There are three steps to the Dream Control we teach, all involving a meditational level of mind.

The first is to learn to recall our dreams. Many say, "I don't dream at all," but that is never true. We may not recall our dreams, but we all dream. Take away our dreams and in a few days mental and emotional troubles set in.

When I began investigating the possible usefulness of dreams in problem solving back in 1949, I was not at all sure what I would find. I had heard, as you have, many stories of premonitions occurring in dreams. Caesar, as we all know, was warned in a dream about the "Ides of March," the very day, as it turned out, when he was assassinated. And Lincoln too dreamed premonitions of his assassination. If these dreams and many others like them were unrepeatable accidents, then I was wasting my time.

At one point I became strongly convinced that I was wasting my time. I had been studying psychology—Freud, Adler, Jung—for about four years, and it began to appear that the more I studied, the less I knew. It was about two A.M. I tossed my book to the floor and went to bed, determined to waste no more time on useless projects like studying the giants who disagreed even among themselves. From now on it would be my electronics business and nothing else. I was neglecting it and money was short.

About two hours later I was awakened by a dream. It was not a series of events, like most dreams, but simply a light. My field of dream vision was filled with midday sunlight, gold, very bright. I opened my eyes and it was dark in my shadowy bedroom. I closed my eyes and it was bright again. I repeated this several times: eyes open, dark; eyes closed, bright. About the third or fourth time my eyes were closed I saw three numbers: 3–4–3. Then another set of numbers: 3–7–3. And the next time the first set came back, and the time after that the second set.

I was less interested in the six numbers than in the

light, which began to fade little by little. I wondered if life came to an end, like an electric bulb, in a sudden flash of light. When I realized I was not dying I wanted to bring the light back to study it. I changed my breathing, my position in bed, my level of mind; nothing worked. It continued to fade. Altogether, the light lasted about five minutes.

Perhaps the numbers had a meaning. I lay awake the rest of the night trying to recall telephone numbers, addresses, license numbers—anything that might give meaning to those numbers.

Today I have an effective way of finding out what dreams mean, but in those days I was still in the early stages of research. The following day, tired as I was after only two hours' sleep, I kept trying to connect the numbers to something I already knew.

Now I must recount some trivial incidents, which led to the unraveling of the mystery and thence to an important part of the Mind Control course.

Fifteen minutes before closing time at my electronics shop, a friend dropped in to suggest we go out for coffee. While he waited for me, my wife came by and said, "As long as you're going for coffee, why not go over to the Mexican side and pick up some rubbing alcohol for me?" Near the bridge there is a store where rubbing alcohol is cheaper.

On the way, I told my friend about the dream, and while I was telling him, an idea occurred to me: Maybe what I saw was a lottery ticket number. We drove past a store which was headquarters for the Mexican lottery, but it was closing time and the shades were already pulled down. No matter, it was a silly idea anyway, and we drove a block farther to buy the alcohol for my wife.

As the salesman wrapped the alcohol for me, my

friend called from another part of the store. "What was that number you were looking for?"

"Three—seven—three, three—four—three," I said.

"Come look!"

There was half a ticket with 3—4—3 on it.

Throughout the Republic of Mexico each of the hundreds of thousands of vendors, like this little store, receives tickets with the same first three numbers every month. This store was the only one in the entire nation which sold number 343. The number 373 was sold in Mexico City.

A few weeks later I learned that my half of the first lottery ticket I ever bought had won $10,000, which I sorely needed. As elated as I was, I looked this gift horse carefully in the mouth, and what I found was more valuable by far than the gift itself. It was foundation for a solidly based conviction that my studies were worthwhile. Somehow I had made contact with Higher Intelligence. Maybe I had made contact with it many times before and not known; this time I *knew*.

Consider the number of seemingly chance events that led to this. In a moment of despair, I dreamed of a number in so startling a way—with the light—that I *had* to recall it. Then a friend dropped in to invite me for coffee and, tired as I was, I accepted. My wife came by and asked me to bring rubbing alcohol, which led me to the only place in Mexico where that particular ticket was on sale.

Anyone who thinks all this is just coincidence would be hard put to explain an amazing, thoroughly checkable fact: Four Mind Control graduates in the United States, using different techniques, which I developed later, also won lotteries. They are Regina M. Fornecker, of Rockford, Illinois, who won $300,000; David Sikich, of Chicago, who won $300,000; Frances Morroni, of

Chicago, who won $50,000; and John Fleming, of Buffalo, New York, who won $50,000.

We have no objection to the word "coincidence" in Mind Control; in fact we attach special meaning to it. When a series of events that is hard to explain leads to a constructive result, we call it coincidence. When they lead to a destructive result, we call it accident. In Mind Control we learn how to trigger coincidences. "Just a coincidence" is a phrase we do not use.

My lottery-winning dream convinced me of the existence of Higher Intelligence and of its ability to communicate with me. That it did so while I was asleep and profoundly disturbed about my life's work is not at all remarkable as I see it now. Thousands of others have received information in their dreams in some paranormal way when they were in despair or danger or at turning points in their lives. Many such dreams are recorded in the Bible. However, at the time, the fact that it happened to *me* seemed like nothing less than a miracle.

I remembered from my readings that Freud said sleep creates favorable conditions for telepathy. To account for my dream I had to go further and say that sleep creates favorable conditions for receiving information from Higher Intelligence. Then I went still further and wondered if we had to be like someone waiting passively for the telephone to ring. Could we not dial the number ourselves to communicate with Higher Intelligence on our own initiative? As a religious person, I reasoned that if we can reach God through prayer, surely we can develop a method for reaching Higher Intelligence. (As you will see later, in Chapter Fifteen, where I speak of God and Higher Intelligence, I am speaking of different things.)

* * *

Yes, my experiments showed that we can reach Higher Intelligence in several ways. One of them is Dream Control, which is very simple and easily learned.

You cannot count on bright lights to help you recall dreams, but you can count on the cumulative effect of programming yourself, while at your level, to remember them. While meditating just before going to sleep, say, "I want to remember a dream. I will remember a dream." Now go to sleep with paper and pencil by your bedside. When you awaken, whether during the night or in the morning, write down what you remember of a dream. Keep practicing this night after night and your recall will be clearer, more complete. When you are satisfied with your improved skill, you are ready for step two:

During meditation before going to sleep, review a problem that can be solved with information or advice. Be sure that you really care about solving it; silly questions evoke silly answers. Now program yourself with these words: "I want to have a dream that will contain information to solve the problem I have in mind. I will have such a dream, remember it, and understand it."

When you awaken during the night or in the morning, review the dream you recall most vividly and search it for meaning.

As I mentioned earlier, our method of dream interpretation must be different from the Freudian one because we deliberately generate dreams. Therefore, if you happen to be familiar with Freudian dream interpretation, forget about it for the purposes of Mind Control.

Imagine what Freud would make of this dream: A man was in a jungle surrounded by savages. They were coming menacingly close to him, their spears rising, then descending. Each spear had a hole in the tip. When he awoke he saw this dream as the answer to a problem that had had him stymied: how to design a sewing machine. He could make the needle rise and descend, but not sew—until his dream told him to put the hole at the tip. The man was Elias Howe, who invented the first practical sewing machine.

A Mind Control graduate credits dream control with saving his life. On the eve of a seven-day motorcycle trip, he programmed a dream to warn him beforehand of any particular danger he might face. Most previous long trips had been marked by small mishaps—a flat tire once; another time dirt in the fuel line; and on his last trip, unforeseen snow.

He dreamed he was at the home of a friend. For dinner he was served a heaping platter of raw string beans, while everyone else enjoyed a delicious quiche Lorraine. Did this mean he was to avoid eating raw string beans on the trip? There was little danger of this, since he dislikes string beans, particularly raw ones. Did it mean he was no longer welcome at his friend's home? No, he was confident of their friendship; besides, that had nothing to do with his motorcycle trip.

Two days later he was speeding along a New York highway at dawn. It was a beautiful morning, the highway was in perfect condition, and there was no traffic except for a small truck ahead.

As he neared the truck he saw that it was loaded with bushels of string beans. Recalling his dream, he slowed down from 65 to 25; then, as he rounded a turn at 15 miles per hour, his rear wheel skidded a little on the turn—on some string beans that had spilled from the truck! At a higher speed the skid would have been serious, possibly fatal.

Only you can interpret the dreams you *decide* to have. With proper self-programming beforehand to understand your dreams, you will have a "hunch" about their meaning. The hunch is often the way our voiceless subconscious communicates with us. With practice you will develop more and more confidence in these programmed hunches.

The words I have suggested you use for self-programming are those we use in Mind Control classes. Other words will work too, but in case you ever take a Mind Control course, you will already be conditioned and will have a richer experience if you have implanted the exact words beforehand while at Alpha.

If you will be patient with Dream Control and practice, you will uncover one of your more priceless mental resources. You would not reasonably expect to become a lottery winner; it is in the nature of lotteries that very few win. But it is in the nature of life that everyone can win much more than lotteries offer.

CHAPTER EIGHT

YOUR WORDS HAVE POWER

In the Introduction it was suggested that you not practice any of the exercises on first reading. The following is an exception; try it right now. Bring all of your imagination to bear on it.

Let's consider the implications of this.

Imagine that you are standing in your kitchen holding a lemon that you have just taken from the refrigerator. It feels cold in your hand. Look at the outside of it, its yellow skin. It is a waxy yellow, and the skin comes to small green points at the two ends. Squeeze it a little and feel its firmness and its weight.

Now raise the lemon to your nose and smell it. Nothing smells quite like a lemon, does it? Now cut the lemon in half and smell it. The odor is stronger. Now bite deeply into the lemon and let the juice swirl around in your mouth. Nothing tastes quite like a lemon either, does it?

At this point, if you have used your imagination well, your mouth will be watering.

Let's consider the implications of this.

Words, "mere" words, affected your salivary glands. The words did not even reflect reality, but something you imagined. When you read those words about the lemon you were telling your brain you had a lemon, though you did not mean it. Your brain took it seriously and said to your salivary glands, "This guy is biting a lemon. Hurry, wash it away." The glands obeyed.

Most of us think the words we use reflect meanings and that what they mean can be good or bad, true or false, powerful or weak. True, but that is only half of it. Words do not just reflect reality, they create reality, like the flow of saliva.

The brain is no subtle interpreter of our intentions— it receives information and stores it, and it is in charge of our bodies. Tell it something like "I'm now eating a lemon," and it goes to work.

Now it is time for what in Mind Control we call "mental housecleaning." There is no exercise for this, just a determination to be careful about what words we use to trigger our brains.

The exercise we did was a neutral one—physically, no good or harm came of it. But good as well as harm can come from the words we use.

Many children play a little game at dinner. They describe the food they are eating in the most nauseating possible terms: Butter is mashed bugs, to choose one of the less colorful ones I remember. The object of the game is to pretend not to be nauseated by these new perspectives on food and to push someone else beyond his ability to pretend. It often works, with someone's appetite suddenly dulled.

As adults we often play this same game. We dull our appetite for life with negative words, and the words, gathering power with repetition, in turn create negative lives, for which our appetites become dulled.

"How are you?"

"Ah—can't complain," or "No use complaining," or "Not too bad."

How does the brain respond to these dreary views?

Is it a "pain in the neck" to do the dishes? Is it "one big headache" to balance your checkbook? Are you "sick and tired" of the weather we are having? I am convinced that proctologists owe a large part of their income to the words we use. Remember, the brain is no subtle interpreter. It says, "This guy's asking for a headache. Okay. One headache coming up."

Of course, every time that we say something gives us a pain, a pain does not immediately result. The body's natural state is good health, and all its processes are geared toward health. In time, though, with enough verbal pounding away at its defenses, it delivers up the very illnesses we order.

Two things add power to the words we use: our level of mind, and our degree of emotional involvement with what we say.

"My God, that hurts!" spoken with conviction offers warm hospitality to pain. "I can't get a damned thing done around here!" said with deep feeling becomes a truth which adds seeming validity to the feeling.

Mind Control offers effective defenses against our own bad habits. At Alpha and Theta our words have enormously increased power. In earlier chapters you have seen how, with amazingly simple words, you can preprogram dreams and transfer from words to your three fingers the power to take you into Alpha.

I never laughed at Emile Coué, though in these sophisticated times many do. He is famous for a sentence which nowadays evokes laughter as reliably as the punch line of a joke: "Day by day, in every way, I am getting better and better." These words have cured thousands of persons of grimly serious illnesses! They are no joke; I respect them and I regard Dr. Coué with awe and gratitude, for I have learned priceless lessons from his book *Self-Mastery Through Autosuggestion* (New York: Samuel Weiser, 1974).

Dr. Coué was a chemist for almost thirty years in Troyes, France, where he was born. After studying and experimenting with hypnosis, he developed a psychotherapy of his own, based on autosuggestion. In 1910 he opened a free clinic in Nancy, where he successfully treated thousands of patients, some with rheumatism, severe headaches, asthma, paralysis of a limb, others with stammering, tubercular sores, fibrous tumors, and ulcers —an amazing variety of afflictions. He never cured anyone, he said; he taught them to cure themselves. There is no doubt that the cures occurred—they are well documented—but the Coué method has almost entirely disappeared since his death in 1926. Had this method been so complex that only a few specialists could learn to practice it, it might be alive and well today. It is a simple method. Everyone can learn it. The heart of it is in Mind Control.

There are two basic principles:

1. We can think of only one thing at a time, and
2. When we concentrate on a thought, the thought becomes true because our bodies transform it into action.

Therefore, if you want to trigger your body's healing processes, which may be blocked by negative thoughts (conscious or unconscious), just repeat twenty times in succession, "Day by day, in every way, I am getting better and better." Do this twice a day and you are using the Coué method.

Since my own research has shown that the power of words is greatly amplified at meditative levels, I have made some adaptations of this method. At Alpha and Theta levels we say, "Every day, in every way, I am getting better, better, *and* better." We say it only once during meditation. We also say—and this too is Dr. Coué's influence—"Negative thoughts, negative suggestions, have no influence over me at any level of mind."

These two sentences alone have produced an impressive number of concrete results. Of particular interest is the experience of a soldier who was suddenly shipped to Indochina before he could complete more than the first day of the Mind Control course. He remembered how to meditate and he remembered these two sentences.

He was assigned to the unit of an alcoholic sergeant with a fiery temper, who singled out the new arrival for special abuse. In a few weeks he began to awaken during the night with fits of coughing, then with attacks of asthma, which he had never had before. An exhaustive medical examination showed that he was in perfect health. Meanwhile he grew more and more tired; he began to perform poorly at his job; and he attracted even more unpleasant attention from his sergeant.

Others in his unit were turning to drugs; he turned to Mind Control and these two sentences. Fortunately he was able to meditate three times a day. "In three days, I had complete immunity to that sergeant. I did what he told me to do, but nothing he said could reach me. In a week I stopped coughing and my asthma was gone."

If this had been told to me by a Mind Control graduate, I would have been pleased, as I always am with success stories, but not strongly impressed. We have a number of more powerful techniques for self-healing, which I will help you learn in later chapters. What makes this man's experience particularly interesting is that he knew none of these techniques, but used only the two sentences he learned that first day.

Words are astonishingly powerful even at levels of mind far deeper than we use in Mind Control. A nurse-anesthetist (and Mind Control lecturer) in Oklahoma, Mrs. Jean Mabrey, puts this knowledge to use to help her patients. As soon as they are "under"—in deep anesthesia—she whispers in their ears instructions that can speed their recovery, in some cases save their lives.

During one operation, when profuse bleeding would normally be expected, the surgeon was amazed: There was only a trickle. Mrs. Mabrey had whispered, "Tell your body not to bleed." She did this before the first incision, then about every ten minutes during the operation.

During another operation she whispered, "When you awaken you will feel that everyone in your life loves you and you will love yourself." This patient was causing her surgeon special concern. She was a tense, complaining woman to whom every pain was ominous—an attitude that could slow down her recovery. Later, as she awakened from the anesthetic, there was a new expression on her face, and three months later her surgeon told Mrs. Mabrey that this once-anxious patient was "transformed." She had become relaxed and optimistic and quickly recovered from her operation.

Mrs. Mabrey's work illustrates three things that we teach in Mind Control: First, words have special power at deep levels of mind; second, the mind has much firmer command over the body than it is given credit for; and third, as I noted in Chapter 5, we are always conscious.

How many parents brusquely pop into a sleeping child's room, quickly adjust the covers, and leave, when a pause for a few positive and loving words would help make the child more secure and calm during the day?

So many Mind Control graduates report improvement in their health, sometimes before they have even completed the course, that I once found myself uncomfortably close to being in trouble with the medical profession in my home town. Some patients told their physicians that we had cured their health problems, and the physicians complained to the District Attorney. He investigated and found that we were not practicing medicine as the doctors feared. Fortunately it is not illegal for Mind Control to be good for the health or there would be no Mind Control organization today.

CHAPTER NINE

THE POWER OF IMAGINATION

Willpower needs an enemy to overcome before it reaches its goal. It tries to be tough and, like most toughies, it becomes a cream puff when the going gets rocky. There is a gentler, easier way to shuck bad habits—imagination. Imagination seizes directly on the goal; it gets what it wants.

This is why in earlier chapters I placed so much emphasis on your learning true-to-life visualization at deep levels of mind. If you spur your imagination with belief, desire, and expectancy, and train it to visualize your goals so that you see, feel, hear, taste, and touch them, you will get what you want.

"When the will and the imagination are in conflict, it is always the imagination that wins," wrote Emile Coué.

If you think you want to give up a bad habit, chances are you are deceiving yourself. If you really wanted to give it up, it would fade away on its own. What you should want more than the habit itself is the benefit of giving it up. Once you learn to want that benefit strongly enough, you will become free of the "unwanted" habit.

Thinking about your habit and firmly resolving to give it up may bind you more tightly to it. It is a little like firmly resolving to go to sleep; the very firmness of your resolve can keep you awake.

Now let's see how all this can be made to work for you. As examples, I will use two habits which Mind Control graduates overcome most successfully: overeating and smoking.

If you want to lose weight, your first step is to reason out the problem at the outer level.

Is your problem overeating, underexercising, or both?

It may very well not be overeating, but eating the wrong foods. A diet of foods more suitable to your particular needs may be the answer. Your physician would know.

Why do you want to lose weight? Are you so fat that your health is impaired, or do you simply feel that a slimmer you would be more attractive? Either provides a good reason for losing weight, but you must know beforehand how you expect to profit from the weight loss.

If you already eat the right foods in modest amounts, if you get as much exercise as you reasonably can, and you are only slightly overweight, my advice would be —unless your physician says otherwise—to live with it. I do. The alternative is an unnecessary disruption for you. Besides, there are probably bigger problems and more important opportunities in your life to put your Mind Control to work on.

If you are sure that you really want to lose weight and you know why, your next step is to analyze all the benefits you will derive—not general benefits like "I'll look better" but concrete ones involving, if possible, all the five senses. Example:

Sight: Find a photograph of yourself when you were as thin as you would like to be now.

Touch: Imagine, when you are thin again, how smooth your arms and thighs and stomach will feel to your touch.

Taste: Imagine the flavors of the foods you will emphasize in your new diet.

Smell: Imagine the odor of the foods you will be eating.

Hearing: Imagine what those who are important to you will say about your success at losing weight!

Even the five senses are not enough for thorough visualization. Emotions are important, too.

Imagine how elated and confident you will feel when you are as thin as you want to be.

With all this firmly in mind, go to your level. Create your mental screen and project onto it a visualization as you are now. Now let it disappear and from the left (the future) slide on an image (the old photograph perhaps) of yourself as you ultimately want to be and will be when the diet succeeds.

While you mentally gaze at the new you, imagine in as much detail as you can what it will feel like to be this thin. How will it feel when you bend over to tie your shoelaces? Walk upstairs? Fit into clothing that is now too small? Walk on a beach in a bathing suit? Take your time and feel all this. Go through the five senses, one at a time, as described above. How will your attitude toward yourself *feel* as a result of achieving this goal?

Now mentally review your new diet—not just what you will eat, but how much—and select a few between-meal snacks, raw carrot or whatever. Tell yourself that this is all the food your body will need and that it will not send you hunger pangs as a way of asking for more.

This is the end of your meditation. Repeat it twice a day.

Notice that not once during your meditation was there any image or thought of the foods you should not eat. You eat too much of them because you like them; the mere thought of them will make your imagination lurch in unwanted directions.

Hollywood actress Alexis Smith was quoted by the San Jose *Mercury News* (October 13, 1974) as saying, "Positive thinking works beautifully on a reducing diet. Never think once about what you are giving up but concentrate on what you are getting." She is often told that she is more attractive now than when she made some of the Warner Brothers movies now showing on TV. She attributes much of this to Mind Control. "The big difference," she is quoted as saying, "is that now I'm in better balance and more in control of myself."

In your weight-loss program, be sure to select a reasonable target for weight reduction; otherwise you will destroy the believability of your project. If you are 50 pounds overweight, you cannot reasonably believe you will look like Audrey Hepburn or Mark Spitz next week. To visualize this will do little good.

Old body messages may come through the first few days to remind you of the delights of a candy bar. During your busy day, when you may be unable to meditate, take a deep breath, put your three fingers together, and remind yourself in the same words you used during meditation that your diet is all your body needs and that you will not have hunger pangs. A quick glance at an old photograph of yourself as you would like to be again will be helpful.

As you progress with your Mind Control in this and other areas, your total mental state will improve and this in turn will contribute in important ways to better functioning of your body. With a little mental nudging it will more gladly seek its proper weight.

There are a number of variations on this technique

that you can use. They may occur to you during meditation. One man, a factory worker in Omaha, said to himself during his meditations, "I will desire and eat only those foods good for my body." Suddenly he found a new interest in salads and vegetable juices and a fading interest in high-calorie foods. Result: He lost 40 pounds in four months.

A woman in Ames, Iowa, used the same technique. A few days later she bought some doughnuts—three for her children and three for their friends. "I completely forgot to buy any for myself. I almost cried. Mind Control was working!"

A farmer in Mason City, Iowa, bought a $150 suit which, to say the least, was a poor fit. He could neither draw up the trousers nor button the jacket. "The salesman thought I was crazy," he said. But with the mental-screen technique, he lost 45 pounds in four months and "now the suit looks tailor-made for me."

Not all the results are this spectacular—in fact, not all of them should be. However, Caroline de Sandre of Denver and Jim Williams, who is in charge of Mind Control activities in the Colorado area, launched an experimental program which shows the reliability of Mind Control techniques for those who genuinely want to lose weight.

She organized a workshop for 25 Mind Control graduates to meet once a week for a month. Among the 15 who attended all the meetings, the average weight loss was a little more than 4¾ pounds. All lost weight!

A month later, she checked with these 15 and learned that 7 had continued to lose weight, and 8 were holding steady. None had gained weight!

This was not only a painless experience for these graduates, it was a joyous one, Caroline reports. Not only did they lose weight with no hunger pangs or any other discomfort, but they reinforced many Mind Control–acquired skills.

The average weight loss was about what it would have been had they taken one of the more successful weight-reduction courses. Caroline herself had been a lecturer for one of these courses for a year and a half, and was Assistant Food Director of the Swedish Medical Center in Denver—she knows about proper nutrition and weight control.

She plans to continue this workshop and to develop another one for smokers.

Smoking is so serious a habit that if you are a smoker, the time to start becoming a former smoker is now. As with weight reduction, we will take this in easy stages, giving your body plenty of time to learn to obey a totally new kind of instruction from your mind.

There is no need for reviewing at the outer level why you should stop; the melancholy reasons are familiar enough. What you need is a list of benefits which you later make so vivid that you will want to stop.

You will have more vitality; your physical senses will be sharper; and you will savor life more fully. You know better than I, a nonsmoker, what you will gain.

Go to your level and see yourself on your mental screen in the situation where you normally smoke your first cigarette of the day. Visualize yourself, fully at ease, from that moment until the end of an hour, doing everything you would normally do except smoking. If, for example, the hour is 7:30 to 8:30 A.M., say to yourself, "I am now and will remain a former smoker from 7:30 to 8:30 A.M. I enjoy being a former smoker during this hour. It is easy and I am used to it."

Continue this exercise until you are really fully at ease, at the outer level, with your first hour of freedom from cigarettes. Now for the next hour, and soon the third, and so on. Take this slowly—pushing too fast may lead to punishing your own body, which is hardly fair, since your mind, not your body, introduced the habit in the first place. Let your mind do the work through imagination.

Here are a few hints to speed up the day of complete liberation:

Change brands frequently.

During the hours when you are not yet a former smoker, ask yourself each time you reach for a cigarette, "Do I really want this one now?" With surprising frequency the answer is no. Wait until you really want it.

If, during one of your liberated hours, your body intrudes with an apparent "need" for a smoke, take a deep breath, put your three fingers together, and—using the same words you use in meditation—remind yourself that you are and will remain a nonsmoker during this hour.

In controlling the smoking habit, you can add other techniques to this basic method. A pack-and-a-half-a-day smoker for eight years, an Omaha man visualized in Alpha all the cigarettes he'd ever smoked—a great heap of them. Then he put them in an incinerator and burned them.

Next he imagined all the cigarettes he would smoke in the future unless he stopped—another great mound of them—and he gleefully burned these too in the incinerator. After having quit smoking many times in the past, this time he gave up cigarettes for good after only one meditation. No craving, no overeating, no side effects.

I cannot, I regret to say, report as much success with smoking as with weight reduction. However, I know of enough graduates who have given up smoking, and enough others who have reduced the amount they smoke, to urge anyone who now smokes to put Mind Control to work on the habit.

CHAPTER TEN

USING YOUR MIND TO
IMPROVE YOUR HEALTH

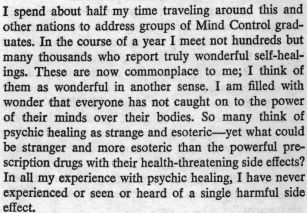

I spend about half my time traveling around this and other nations to address groups of Mind Control graduates. In the course of a year I meet not hundreds but many thousands who report truly wonderful self-healings. These are now commonplace to me; I think of them as wonderful in another sense. I am filled with wonder that everyone has not caught on to the power of their minds over their bodies. So many think of psychic healing as strange and esoteric—yet what could be stranger and more esoteric than the powerful prescription drugs with their health-threatening side effects? In all my experience with psychic healing, I have never experienced or seen or heard of a single harmful side effect.

Medical research is finding out more and more about the relationship between the body and the mind. Of all the different, seemingly unrelated research efforts, there is a fascinating consistency about the findings: The mind turns out to play a mysteriously powerful role.

If Mind Control were perfect (it is not; we are still learning) I believe we would all have perfect bodies, all the time. However, it is an inescapable fact that we already know enough to strengthen with our minds the body's repair forces so that illnesses can be combatted more successfully. Even the simple methods of Emile Coué worked. Mind Control's methods, which include Coué's, work even more powerfully.

Obviously, as you develop more skill in self-healing you will require less medical attention. However, at this stage in the development of Mind Control, and at this stage in your mastery of what we have developed, it is far too early for the nation's physicians to go into retirement. What you *should* do is consult them, as you would normally, and follow their advice. What you *can* do is amaze them with the speed of your recovery. Someday they may wonder where you went.

Many graduates report they use Mind Control in emergencies to reduce bleeding and pain. Example: Mrs. Donald Wildowsky was in Texas on a convention trip with her husband. According to the Norwich, Connecticut, *Bulletin,* she dived into a swimming pool and ruptured an eardrum.

"We were miles from any town, and I didn't want to make him leave in the middle of the convention," she was quoted as saying. "So I went to an Alpha state, put my hand over my ear, concentrated on the pain area and said 'Gone, gone, gone!'

"The bleeding stopped immediately and the pain left. When I finally got to a doctor, he was speechless with amazement."

In self-healing, there are six fairly easy steps to take.

The first is to begin—in Beta—to feel yourself becoming a loving (and therefore a forgiving) person, and to consider love as an end in itself. This will probably require a pretty thorough mental housecleaning (see Chapter 8).

Second, go to your level. This alone is a major step

toward self-healing because, as I mentioned much earlier, at this level the negative work of the mind—all its guilts and angers—is neutralized, and the body is set free to do what nature designed it to do: repair itself. You may, of course, have very real feelings of guilt and anger, but we have found that these will be experienced only at the outer, or Beta, level and they tend to disappear as you practice Mind Control.

Third, mentally speak to yourself about step one: Express your desire to achieve a thorough mental housecleaning—to use positive words, to think positively, to become a loving, forgiving person.

Fourth, mentally experience the illness that is troubling you. Use the mental screen and see and feel the illness. This should be brief; its purpose is simply to focus your healing energies where they are needed.

Fifth, quickly erase this image of your illness and experience yourself as completely cured. Feel the freedom and happiness of being in perfect health. Hold on to this image, linger over it, enjoy it, and know that you deserve it—know that now in this healthy state you are fully in tune with nature's intentions for you.

Sixth, reinforce your mental housecleaning once again, and end by saying to yourself, "Every day in *every* way I am getting better, better, *and* better."

How long should this take and how often should you do it?

My experience is that fifteen minutes is about the best length of time. Go through this exercise as often as you can, no less often than once a day. There is no "too much."

Allow me to digress for a moment. You may have heard that meditation is a fine thing but that you must be careful not to become so enchanted by it that you do too much. This, it is said, can lead to a withdrawal from the world and an unhealthy preoccupation with yourself. Whether this is true or not, I do not know. This is said of other meditative disciplines, not Mind Control. Our emphasis is on involvement with the world, not withdrawal from it—not with transcending practical problems or ignoring them, but with facing them head-on and solving them. You cannot do too much of this.

To return to self-healing: There is no end to step one. Practice it in Beta, Alpha, and Theta. Live it. If you feel it slipping during the day, put your three fingers together for instant reinforcement.

Many of our Mind Control centers publish newsletters for their graduates. These are filled with reports from graduates on what Mind Control has done for them. Stories of how they control headaches, asthma, fatigue, and high blood pressure are too numerous to count.

Here is one, which I select because the author is a practicing physician.

From the time I was about eleven I had migraine headaches. At first they occurred occasionally and could be controlled, but then as I grew older they became worse and finally I was having "cluster headaches" lasting three or four days, with only a two-day interval between attacks. A full-blown migraine is devastating . . . usually involving one side of the face and head. The eyes feel as if they were being pushed out of their sockets. The pain is vise-like and the stomach turns somersaults. The attack is sometimes relieved by a specific preparation, a vasoconstricting drug, which has to be taken at the onset while the pain is tolerable. Once the headache has progressed for some time there is nothing that will relieve it except time. I was getting to the point where I had to take the preparation every four hours and even then the relief was only partial.

So I went to a headache specialist, who gave me a complete examination to be certain that I didn't have any physical or neurological abnormalities. He gave me advice and treatment which I had already been practicing; the headaches continued.

One of my patients was a Mind Control graduate, and for about a year she'd been suggesting I go with her to Mind Control. I always told her I didn't believe in that nonsense. Then one day I saw her on about the fourth day of a headache and I must have been looking green and she said, "Isn't it about time you took Mind Control? There's a new course starting next week . . . why don't you come along with me?"

I signed up for the course and went faithfully every single night, and sure enough, I didn't have a headache that week. But a week after I finished the course I woke up with a terrible headache and a chance to see whether my programming would work. I went through one cycle and counted out . . . no headache . . . felt great. It was a miracle! Five seconds later the headache came back even worse. I didn't give up, so I did another cycle, and the headache momentarily went away, then came back again. I had to go through about ten cycles, but I kept it up and didn't take migraine medication. I told myself I was going to do it, and the headache finally did go away.

I didn't have a headache for a while, but the next time three cycles relieved it. I had headaches off and on for about three months after that, but I didn't even need to take an aspirin. Since I took Mind Control I haven't taken an aspirin. It really works!

Here is another, from a nun, Sister Barbara Burns of Detroit, Michigan. I select this one because Sister Barbara has made ingenious use of her own triggering mechanism.

For twenty-seven years she had worn glasses because of nearsighted astigmatism. As her nearsightedness increased, her lenses were made stronger, which reduces distance acuity. Before the improvement of her eyesight, bifocals became necessary. Then, in July 1974, she decided to use Mind Control. In deep meditation she told herself, "Every time I blink my eyes, they will focus accurately, like the lens of a camera." During each meditation she repeated this, and in two weeks she began to live without glasses, though she still needed them for reading. She consulted Dr. Richard Wlodyga, an optometrist (and Mind Control graduate), who told her that her cornea was slightly misshapen. Sister Barbara inserted the cornea correction into her meditation for the few weeks' interval before another examination by Dr. Wlodyga.

The following is part of a letter to us from Dr. Wlodyga, which Sister Barbara asked him to write:

Sister Barbara Burns was first examined by me on 20 August 1974. . . .

I examined Sister Burns again on 26 August 1975. She had not worn her glasses for one year. . . .

[The] patient has had a reduction in the amount of manifest myopia to a level where glasses have become unnecessary.

Of course the physician with migraine and Sister Barbara Burns were not suffering from "dread diseases" of the kind we are trained to fear. Can Mind Control help if one of these should strike, or must we simply take our medicine and wait for time to pass? Let us take a look at what is probably the most feared disease of all, cancer.

You may have read about the work of Dr. O. Carl Simonton, a cancer specialist. Marilyn Ferguson described some of it in her recent popular book *The Brain Revolution,* and in January 1976, *Prevention Magazine* published an article about him, "Mind Over Cancer," by Grace Halsell. Dr. Simonton, who was trained in Mind Control techniques, has successfully adapted some of these to treating his patients.

When he was in charge of radiation therapy at Travis Air Force Base near San Francisco he studied a rare but well-known phenomenon: persons who, for no reason known to medicine, recover from cancer. These are known as "spontaneous remissions," and they constitute a very small percentage of all cancer patients. If he could learn why these patients recovered, Dr. Simonton reasoned, perhaps he could find a way to cause remissions to occur.

He found that these patients had something very important in common. They were often positive, optimistic, determined people.

In an address at the Boston Convention of Mind Control in 1974, he said:

The biggest single emotional factor identified by investigators in the development of cancer in general is a significant loss six to eighteen months prior to the diagnosis of the disease.

This has been shown in several long-term studies by independent investigators with control groups. . . . We see that it is not just that loss that is a significant factor, but it is the way that loss is received by the individual.

You see, the loss has to be sufficient to cause a feeling of helplessness and hopelessness that persists on the part of the patient. Thus, it would seem that his basic resistance goes down, allowing the malignancy to develop clinically.

In another study at Travis Air Force Base, reported in the *Journal of Transpersonal Psychology,** Dr. Simonton rated the attitudes of 152 cancer patients in five categories, from strongly negative to strongly positive. Then he rated their responses to therapy, from excellent to poor. For 20 of these patients, results of their treatment were excellent—though the condition of 14 of them was so serious they would have had less than a fifty-percent chance of living five years. What tipped the balance was their positive attitudes. At the other end of the scale, 22 showed poor results from the treatment; none of these had positive attitudes.

However, when some of the more positive patients returned home there was a turnaround in their attitudes, "and we saw their disease change correspondingly." Clearly, their attitudes rather than the severity of their illness played the stronger role.

Dr. Elmer Green of the Menninger Foundation was quoted by the *Journal's* editor as saying, "Carl and Stephanie Simonton are . . . getting remarkable results in cancer control by coupling visualization for physiological self-regulation with traditional radiology."

In his Boston speech, Dr. Simonton quoted the President of the American Cancer Society, Eugene Pendergrass, who said in 1959, "There is some evidence that

---

* Vol. 7, no. 1, 1975.

the course of disease in general is affected by emotional distress. It is my sincere hope that we can widen the quest to include the distinct possibility that within one's mind is a power capable of exerting forces which can either enhance or inhibit the progress of this disease."

Dr. Simonton is now Medical Director of the Cancer Counseling and Research Center in Fort Worth, where he and his co-therapist, Stephanie Mathews-Simonton, train patients to participate mentally in their own treatment.

"You see, I began with the idea that a patient's attitude played a role in his response to any form of treatment and could influence the course of his disease. As I explored this, I found that Mind Control—biofeedback and meditation—concepts gave me a tool to use in teaching the patient how to begin the interaction and become involved with his own health process. I would say that it is the most powerful single tool that I have to offer the patient emotionally."

One of the first steps Dr. Simonton takes in training his patients is to banish fear. Once this education is begun, "we realize that cancer is a normal process going on in all of us, that we have cancerous cells developing malignant degeneration all the time. The body recognizes and destroys them the way it handles any foreign protein. . . . It is not simply a matter of getting rid of all the cancer cells, because we develop cancer cells all the time. It is getting the body back winning again, handling its own processes."

Dr. Simonton's address was followed by one from Mrs. Simonton. She said:

> Most people . . . visualize a cancer cell as being a very ugly, mean, insidious thing that can sneak around and is very powerful; once it gets started there is nothing the body can do. In reality a

cancer cell is a normal cell that has gone crazy. . . . It is a very stupid cell—it reproduces so rapidly that many times it will encompass its own blood supply and starve itself. It is weak. You cut into it, or radiate it, or give it chemotherapy, and if it gets sick at all, it can't regain its health. It dies.

Now compare that to a healthy cell. We know that in healthy tissue you can cut your finger, and if you do nothing more than put a Band-Aid on it, it will heal itself. We know that normal tissues can repair themselves . . . they don't devour their own blood supply. Yet look at the mental image we have of those things. You can see the power we ascribe to the disease by our fears and the mental imagery we use in our fears.

Referring to the relaxation and visualization techniques they use along with radiation therapy, Mrs. Simonton said:

Probably the single most valuable tool we have is the mental imagery technique.

There are three basic things we ask patients to do. We ask them to visualize their disease, visualize their treatment, and to visualize the body's immune mechanism.

[In our group sessions] what we talk about is picturing what we want to come about. Before we believe it will come about. It seems to be important to picture it that way.

One of the main things we talk about is the meditation. How often are you meditating? What are you doing in your meditation?

CHAPTER ELEVEN

AN INTIMATE EXERCISE FOR LOVERS

In her address before the Mind Control group, Mrs. Simonton spoke of the many stresses in life which, if not handled properly, can lead to illness.

"It is so uncommon in our patients for them to have a good marriage," she said. "When there is a good marriage with a cancer patient, it is one of the greatest things we have to work with, one of the greatest reasons for them to stay alive."

What makes a good marriage? I do not have all the answers. My own marriage to Paula is an extraordinarily good one—it has been rich and interesting for thirty-six years, but I do not thoroughly understand why. Perhaps not thoroughly understanding is part of what makes it good. I say this so you will understand that I have no firsthand experience with unhappy marriage and am therefore no expert on how to rescue one —or whether one should be rescued—when it is in deep trouble.

However, I do know a few ways of enriching and improving a marriage when both husband and wife want this to happen.

You might expect me to speak first of sex, since

many believe it to be the underpinning of a good marriage. I see it more as a result of a good marriage and will discuss it later.

The best foundation for a marriage, I believe, is intimacy—not an invasion-of-privacy kind of intimacy, but the sort that comes from deep understanding and acceptance.

I am about to suggest something rather strange, but I must give you some background first. We have spoken about the lifting joy toward the end of the Mind Control course. Something else occurs, too. It is more subtle but deeply felt. The students, moments away from graduation, feel that they are in intimate, almost loving touch with each other. They came as strangers whose paths might otherwise never have crossed, and they will soon leave to live out their individual destinies. Yet this feeling of connection with one another will easily be reawakened should they meet again.

This is widely believed to stem from the fact that they have been through an intense, once-in-a-lifetime experience together. Soldiers often feel this way after they have shared the intense experiences of war. So too would any group of strangers who found themselves trapped together for an afternoon in an elevator.

This is only part of the explanation, not even the larger part of it. It is the part most often seized upon because it can be easily grasped.

Something else happens, which I shall try to explain. During deep and prolonged meditation, connections are made—minds are sensitively receptive and are gently touched by other minds in ways otherwise familiar only to those who have lived full lifetimes together. Most instant intimacies are superficial and false and leave us feeling a little uncomfortable. They last only briefly. Not this experience; it is on a durable psychic level.

Because it is a subtle feeling rather than an overwhelming one, do not be surprised if you heard nothing of it from any Mind Control graduate you may have met. Mention it and that person will probably say, "Oh, yes. We all felt it. It was beautiful!"

This is a sort of by-product of Mind Control training. The course is not specifically designed to achieve it.

However (this is the strange suggestion I mentioned) it is possible to use what both of you, as husband and wife, have already learned about Mind Control to deliberately create a very comfortable intimacy that only years of living together could otherwise achieve. The result will be stronger and deeper than the one our students experience in classes.

Here is what to do:

1. Select a place where you both feel happiest, most relaxed. It might be a place where you vacationed together, any place with especially pleasant memories you share. It can even be a place neither of you has ever seen—you can create it together. Do not, however, select a place where only one of you has been. This will skew the symmetry of the experience and reduce the sense of sharing.

2. Sit comfortably, close, facing each other. Relax and let your eyes close.

3. One of you will say to the other something like this: "I'm going to count slowly from ten to one, and with each count you will feel yourself going deeper into a pleasant, meditative level of mind. Ten—nine—feel going deeper—eight—seven—six—deeper and deeper —five—four—deeper still—three—two—one. You are now relaxed, at a deep, pleasant level of mind. With your help, I will join you there."

4. The other will say, "I will count slowly from ten to one, and with each count we'll come closer in a deep level of mind. Ten—nine—feel going deeper with

me—eight—seven—six—deeper and deeper together—five—four—deeper still and closer—three—two—one. We are now both relaxed, at a pleasant level of mind. Let us go deeper together."

5. The first person will say, "All right, let's go very deep together. Let's experience our place of relaxation together. The more we experience this, the deeper we will go. Notice the sky . . ."

6. "Yes . . . it's clear, with a few drifting clouds." Each of you will slowly, spontaneously, describe the scene you are experiencing together—the temperature, the colors, the sounds, all the pleasant details.

7. When you are both at a deep level—no hurry about this—and fully experiencing your place of relaxation, one of you will say to the other, "I want most in life to make you happy, and only then do I want to make myself happy."

8. The other will say, "And I want most to make you happy, and only then to make myself happy."

9. Allow a period—as long as you want—of silent communion, then awaken. For some, this period of silent communion may be experienced even more deeply by gazing into each other's eyes. It is entirely possible for the experienced meditator to remain at Alpha or Theta with eyes open. If you are not comfortable with this, do not force it.

This is a far more powerful experience than you might imagine from just reading about it here. The very first time you try it you will be convinced and, with variations you may develop, it may become a permanent part of your lives together.

A few words of caution: The beauty of this experience will be completely lost if it is misused. If one of the two persons involved does not understand the purpose of it and fully agree with that purpose, the resulting sense of intimate communion may come as a less than agreeable experience. I recommend it only for a man and woman seeking a deeper, richer, more durable commitment to each other.

Each of us has an aura which some can see as a faintly visible energy field surrounding the body. We can be trained to see this aura. In fact, as another by-product of Mind Control training, many of our graduates report they see their own and others' auras. Each is as distinctive as a fingerprint.

When people are physically close, their energy fields overlap. Their shape, their intensity, their color, their vibrations change. This happens in crowded theaters and buses as well as in beds with two. The more frequent the contact, the more durable is the change in the auras.

In the case of husband and wife this change is a good one, because their auras become more complementary. Prolonged physical separation will reverse the process, which, needless to say, is not good for the compatibility of the marriage. Physical closeness is essential. I recommend double beds.

Now for sex: Sex is not one experience. There is an entire spectrum of possibilities. I am not speaking of techniques or positions; I mean experiences—qualities of experience at different depths and intensities. There is as wide a range of possibilities as there is between kicks and lasting joy.

Too many couples read how-to-do-it sex manuals and, with a certain perfection of technique, think they are living a good sex life. To deliberate each step, with each step leading logically to the next, keeps what could be a deep experience on the superficial, conscious level of Beta. More important is to flow with the experience, with the mind relaxed, at a meditative level.

Becoming psychically sensitive can enrich and improve a marriage immensely. Even without training, long and happy marriages can result in a deep psychic understanding between partners. Why wait?

CHAPTER TWELVE

YOU <u>CAN</u> PRACTICE ESP

Is ESP real? Today virtually all informed people agree that it is. It has been proved to the last decimal point of probability statistics that information is available to us through something other than the five senses. It can be information from the past, the present, or the future. It can be from a point nearby or far away. Neither time nor space nor Faraday cages are a barrier to whatever "extrasensory" faculty is at work in ESP.

ESP stands for "extrasensory perception." I do not like this terminology. "Extrasensory" means outside, apart from, our sensory apparatus. This seems to deny the existence of a sensory apparatus other than the five senses, though obviously one exists, since we do sense information without the use of them. There is nothing extrasensory at all about ESP. The word "perception" is fine for the sort of experiments conducted by J. B. Rhine at Duke University, where percipients guessed the turn of special cards accurately enough to virtually rule out chance. However, in Mind Control we do not simply perceive, we actually project our awareness to where the desired information is. Perception is too passive a word for what we do. Therefore in Mind Control we speak of "Effective Sensory Projection." The initials are the same, and appropriately so, since we mean all that is generally understood by ESP and more.

To experience ESP, Mind Control students go through no card-guessing exercises. These aim at finding out if people are psychic. We already know they are and we therefore set ourselves a larger task—to train them to perform psychically with real life in ways so exciting that they experience a sort of spiritual "high" so exquisitely intense that their lives are never quite the same again. This comes at the end of about forty hours of instruction and exercises.

We routinely and reliably train people to function psychically; we have done so with over a half-million graduates.

By the time you have mastered all the techniques so far in this book, you will be well on your way to practicing ESP. You will be able to enter deep levels of mind and remain fully conscious, and you will be able to visualize things and events almost with the fullness of five-senses reality. These are the two gateways to the psychic world.

In Mind Control classes students are close to operating psychically by the end of the second day, and on the third they actually do operate psychically—to project their awareness outside their bodies.

They begin with a simple exercise in visual imagination. In very deep meditation they project themselves in front of their own homes by *imagining* they are there. They carefully note everything they see before they enter by the front door to stand in their living room facing the south wall. They see this room at night with the lights on, then in the daytime with sunlight coming through the windows, and study every detail they can remember. Then they touch the south wall and enter it. This may sound outlandish to you, but it is perfectly natural to those who have gone through intensive training in visualization.

Inside the wall they are where they have never been before, so they "test" their new environment by noting the light, the odors, the temperature, and, by knocking on the inside of the wall, the solidity of the materials. Outside the wall again and facing it, they change its color to black, red, green, blue, and violet, then return it to its original color. Next they hold up a chair— weightless in this dimension—and study it against the wall as they change its color again. They do this with a watermelon, a lemon, an orange, three bananas, three carrots, and a head of lettuce.

When this session is completed, the first important step has been taken to put the logical mind in the back seat and the imaginative mind up front where the controls are. In the kind of exercises I am describing now, the logical mind tells the student, "No, don't tell me you're inside a wall or some other outlandish place. You *know* that can't be; you're sitting here."

But the imaginative mind, now strengthened by a series of visualization exercises, is able to ignore this. As the imagination grows even stronger, so do our psychic powers. It is the imaginative mind which holds them.

During the next session the students mentally project themselves into cubes or cylinders of metal—stainless steel, copper, brass, and lead—where, as they did inside the wall, they test for light, odor, color, temperature, and solidity, all at a pace rapid enough to keep logic out of the way.

Working their way up from the simple to the more complex arrangements of matter, they begin their projection into living matter with a fruit tree. They examine a fruit tree in all four seasons against a sequence of colors on their mental screens, then project into the leaves and the fruit.

Now for a giant step forward: projection into a pet. The students have been so successful up to this point that "Can I really do this?" is a question that crosses very few minds. They confidently examine a pet from the outside against their mental screens, with colors changing; then, just as confidently, they mentally enter the skull and living brain. After a few minutes of reconnaissance inside the pet's head, they emerge once again to examine him from the outside, this time focusing on the chest. Now inside the chest to examine the rib cage, the spine, the heart, the lungs, the liver; then out again, now armed with points of reference for what will probably be the most dumbfounding day of their lives, the fourth day, when they will work with humans. However, there is preparatory work to do beforehand.

In an especially deep level of meditation, sometimes well into Theta, Mind Control students—in their now well-trained imaginations—construct laboratories of whatever size, shape, and color they are comfortable with. These will include a desk and chair of their own design, a clock, a calendar containing all dates, past, present, and future, plus filing cabinets. Nothing unusual so far.

To understand the next step it is necessary to point out again how far our psychic sensing apparatus is from language and logic, how close it is to images and symbols. I point this out because the next step is to equip the laboratory with "instruments" for psychically correcting abnormalities detected in the humans who will be examined the following day. Most of these instruments are like nothing you have seen in any laboratory. They are highly instrumental symbols—symbolic instruments, if you will.

Imagine a fine sieve for filtering impurities from

blood; a delicate brush to sweep away the white powder (calcium) that can be seen psychically in cases of arthritis; lotions for fast healing; baths for washing away guilt; a hi-fi set with special music for calming the distressed. Every student makes up his own armamentarium; no two sets of tools are exactly alike. They come from where all is possible, from deep levels of mind, and many graduates come to realize that the work they do with them has consequences in what we call the objective world.

As the student works with these tools, he may have need of some wise counsel to help in perplexing moments—an inner "still small voice." For the Mind Control student, though, it is not a small voice but a strong one, and not one but two.

In his laboratory he evokes two counselors, a man and a woman. He is told before he begins this meditative session that he will do this and, if he is like most other students, he will have a pretty firm idea of whom he wants as counselors. Rarely does he get his wish; almost never is he disappointed.

One student, hoping to meet Albert Einstein, found instead a small man in clown's paint, with a rose-colored Ping-Pong ball for a nose, and wearing a cap with a pinwheel. The little man turned out to be a reliable source of practical advice.

Another student, Sam Merrill, who wrote an article about Mind Control in *New Times* (May 2, 1975), evoked two very real people as counselors, though their behavior was far removed from their real selves.

In his laboratory, the submarine *Nautilus,* writes Merrill, "a little man in knickers and a silk shirt emerged from the decompression chamber. He was slim, balding and gentle, doe-like eyes set in deep sockets. My counselor was William Shakespeare. I said 'Hi' but he didn't answer.

". . . a disembodied voice announced that we were going ashore, and Will and I leapt from a hatchway onto a deserted beach. . . .

"On the beach, we met my second counselor, Sophia Loren. She had just returned from a swim and her cotton T-shirt clung lusciously to the goodies beneath. She too ignored me at first, but was overjoyed to meet Shakespeare. The two shook hands, exchanged pleasantries, then fell to the sand, began thrashing, throbbing, grunting, squealing. . . ."

The next day, when it was time for the serious business of working cases, Mr. Merrill's orientologist gave him the name of a sixty-two-year-old woman in Florida. The two counselors, more interested in each other than the woman, playfully examined her and left to attend to more pressing matters.

Had the counselors left without giving counsel? No—the woman's abdomen had disappeared. "In its place," wrote Merrill, "was a length of pink neon intestine that flashed angrily." He learned from his orientologist that the woman was in the hospital with a seriously inflamed intestine—diverticulitis.

Counselors can be very real to Mind Control graduates. What are they? We are not sure—perhaps some figment of an archetypal imagination, perhaps an embodiment of the inner voice, perhaps something more. What we do know is that, once we meet our counselors and learn to work with them, the association is respectful and priceless.

More than four centuries before Christ, the Greek philosopher Socrates had a counselor who, unlike our counselors in Mind Control, limited his advice to warnings. According to Plato, Socrates said, "I have, since my childhood, been attended by a semi-divine being whose voice from time to time dissuades me from some undertaking, but never directs me what I am to do."

Another writer, Xenophon, quotes Socrates as saying, "up to now the voice has never been wrong."

As you will soon see, a Mind Control graduate, mentally in his laboratory, confidently consulting his counselors, is a person with an immense power to benefit himself and others. At this point in Mind Control training, this is understood but not yet experienced.

The next day the air almost trembles with expectation. Even our graduates who come back to us for a refresher feel it. So far, everything the student has experienced has been apparent only to him, in the privacy of his own mind. Now comes the moment for performing so that everyone can see.

There are two mental exercises beforehand, both mental examinations of the body of a friend, pretty much as was done earlier with pets, but this time in more functional detail. With this completed, the students pair off.

One member of each pair is called the "psychorientologist," and the other the "psychic operator." ("Psychorientologist" is derived from "psychorientology," a word I coined to describe everything we do in Mind Control; it simply means orienting the mind.)

The psychorientologist writes on a card the name of a person he knows, his age, his general whereabouts, and a description of some major physical affliction. The psychic operator, sometimes with the help of his psychorientologist, goes to his level, probably for the first and last time with shaky confidence in what he is about to do.

When he signals that he is ready—at his level, in his laboratory, in the presence of his counselors—the psychorientologist tells him the name, age, sex, and location of the person whose name is on the card. The psychic operator's job is to find out what is wrong with this person he has never met and never heard of until this moment. He examines this person's body, inside and out, in the orderly way his imagination has been trained to do, consulting with his counselors when necessary, perhaps "speaking" to the person himself.

The psychic operator is urged by his psychorientologist to report findings as he goes along, to "keep talking, even if you feel you're guessing." Typically, a session would sound like this (the following is based on a real case):

Psychorientologist: "The name of the person I have listed here is John Summers. He is forty-eight years old, lives in Elkhart, Indiana. One, two, three—John Summers of Elkhart, Indiana, is now on your screen. Sense it, feel it, visualize it, imagine it, create it, know he is there, take it for granted he is there. Scan the body with your intelligence from where you know the head to be to where you know the feet are, up and down, up and down, once a second.

"While scanning the body in this manner, allow your imagination to select the three areas of greatest attraction. Maintain the rate of scanning at once a second and mention to me the areas of attraction as they come to you. You will feel as though you are making it up, so tell me everything that enters your mind."

Psychic operator: "He carries his right shoulder a little lower, a little forward. . . . Everything else seems okay except maybe the left ankle. . . . Let's look inside the chest. . . . Everything's warm . . . a little cooler on the right . . . cooler and darker. . . . His right lung is gone. . . . Now to that ankle. . . . Seems okay, just a little jagged white line there . . . hurts in damp weather . . . must have broken it sometime. . . . I guess that's all. . . . Wait, my female counselor is turning the guy around for me, pointing to a spot behind his ears . . . yes, terribly deep scars there . . . he had a mastoid operation, very deep. . . . Okay, that's all."

Psychorientologist: "Very good. He is missing his right lung and there is a deep scar behind one ear. I have no information about the ankle. Now review the feelings you had when you told me about the right lung and the scar behind the ear. Review your feeling and use this as a point of reference next time you work a case."

After a moment's pause the psychic returns to Beta, smiling. "Wow! That's crazy!"

Yes, it is crazy. It violates everything we have experienced in this sane world. However, there is nothing unusual about this scene I have just described. Some miss a little on their first case, some miss altogether on the first, second, even third case; but as the day draws to an end, virtually everyone has scored enough direct hits to know it is not "just coincidence"—something very real is at work here.

Too often we think of the imagination as an irresponsible creator of nonsense. Often it is. But works of art are the products of trained imaginations; psychic results are also the product of imaginations trained in a very special way. The Mind Control student, when he functions psychically for the first time, feels that he is "just imagining" what he sees. This is why the psychorientologist tells him to "keep talking, even if you feel you are just guessing." If he were to stop talking, his logical mind might tempt him to start reasoning things out, stifling his psychic powers, just as it does in everyday life.

After his first direct hit, the Mind Control student knows he is not "just imagining." He is imagining and learning to trust the first thing that comes to mind. This is his psychic gift coming through.

What is at work are perfectly natural laws. Our minds are not confined to our heads; they reach out. To reach out effectively, they must be motivated by desire, fueled by belief, sparked by expectancy.

On his first case the average student does not have high expectancy. If he is at all informed and open-minded he knows perfectly well there is such a thing as ESP, but his entire life's training has "proved" to him that ESP is someone else's ability, not his. Once he learns differently, once he scores his first hit, his expectancy leaps and he is on his way. A few hours later, with eight or nine other good cases under his belt, he will be a Mind Control graduate.

"Time and again I saw students correctly diagnosing the illness. . . ." wrote Bill Starr of *Midnight* in his article "Mind Control Classes CAN Improve Your Mental Power" (November 19, 1973). In it he described a case he had once presented that he had thought would prove especially difficult to diagnose because neither he nor anyone else in the class knew what the illness was.

Earlier that day, a Mr. Thomas, a Mind Control graduate, had visited his son in the hospital. There was another patient in the room. Thomas learned nothing about him except his name.

Here is what the psychic found: The right leg was "sort of paralyzed," the arms and shoulders were stiff, and some vertebrae in the back were fused because of a disease. In addition, the man had a sore throat and his intestines were inflamed. He was five and a half feet tall and weighed a hundred and five pounds.

Back at the hospital, Mr. Thomas learned that the patient had been a victim of polio in childhood. He had fallen from a wheelchair and broken his right hip, and everything else the Mind Control student said was correct, except for the sore throat and inflamed intestines. Those were his son's symptoms.

Often what appear to be misses turn out, like this one, to be hits on the wrong target. With practice, the aim improves. With more practice, the psychic can connect with things as well as people.

Dick Mazza, an actor-singer in New York, supplements his income by typing book manuscripts for writers and publishers. One day he lost a manuscript and frantically called a Mind Control graduate to help him find it. He had it last, he said, when he entered a small church auditorium to rehearse a play. A group of young morticians were leaving; they were there for graduation exercises. The manuscript was in a white envelope with Dick's name and address and the word "rush" written on it.

The Mind Control graduate has as one of his counselors an elderly mute woman whose usefulness is limited to yes and no nods and a sort of sign language. The male counselor helps out as an interpreter and occasionally pitches in with his own advice.

The graduate visualized the manuscript as Dick described it. He saw it in the middle of a stack of papers on a large, untidy desk.

"Is the manuscript safe there?" he asked his woman counselor. She nodded yes.

"Does one of the new morticians have it?"

No.

"Is the desk in the church?"

No.

"Will it be returned soon?"

Yes.

"Who has it?"

She pointed at the graduate himself. "I have it?" he asked.

No.

The male counselor came to the rescue. "She means someone about your age has it. He asked a young woman to take his papers back to his office because he was going out to celebrate with his students. It's on his desk.

Don't worry, when he sees it, he'll send it along to Dick."

Two days later the dean of the morticians' school telephoned Dick. After the graduation, he explained, he had picked up a stack of his papers that somehow included the manuscript and asked his secretary to put them on his desk because he was going out to have a few drinks with the new graduates.

It has occurred to many that in our case work we are dealing with nothing more than thought transference. (Nothing more! How sophisticated some folks are!)

The case I used as an example—the one of the man with the missing lung—is a real one. You will recall there was one apparent miss, the broken ankle. The orientologist could confirm (he had written them down beforehand) the mastoid operation and the missing lung. But all he could say about the broken ankle was "I have no information about that."

Later the person whose case was being worked confirmed that in fact he had broken his ankle years before, and that it causes him some discomfort in damp weather. Thought transference? Not as we normally understand the term; the thought was not in the mind of the orientologist, for he knew nothing about the broken ankle. Nor was it likely to have been in the mind of the "case" at that moment.

But, you may object, it just might have been in his mind. Yes, it just might have been. Another case: A student doing case work reported that a woman had a scar on her elbow from a fracture. The orientologist had no information about it and checked with the woman, who said no, she had never injured her elbow. Then a few days later the woman mentioned it to her mother.

She had, it turned out, broken her elbow when she was three years old! Is this thought transference?

The psychic energy which people send out is strongest when their survival is at stake. This is why so many cases of spontaneous ESP involve accidents and sudden death.

It is for this reason that our final exercise is case work with severely ill people. The graduate who conscientiously practices his case work learns to pick up weaker and weaker psychic signals until one day he is able psychically to connect with anyone he has in mind, whether or not the person is in trouble. With practice we become more and more sensitive.

In my early experiments I learned that children demonstrate psychic ability more readily than adults do. They are far less limited by Beta's view of what is possible, and their sense of reality has not developed to the point where they will say only those things that seem logical.

One experiment, just after the basics of the Mind Control course were developed, was designed to work out the structure of the case-working sessions I have described. As you will see, my earlier technique was quite different from what it is today.

Two children, Jimmy and Timmy, had been trained in the basics. I separated them, putting each in a different room, each with an experimenter, a sort of forerunner of today's psychorientologist. One child, Jimmy, was asked to go to his level and create something, anything, in his imagination. Meanwhile Timmy, in the other room, went to his level and was asked to find out what Jimmy was up to. Jimmy said to his experimenter, "I'm making a little truck. It has a green body and red wheels."

Timmy's experimenter asked, "What is Jimmy doing now?"

"Oh, he's making a little toy truck."

"Well, describe it."

"Oh, it has a green body and red wheels."

This is case work at a more subtle level than we conduct with adults in our classes. It takes practice to "become as little children."

CHAPTER THIRTEEN

FORM YOUR OWN
PRACTICE GROUP

I want you to come as close as possible, through reading this book, to developing your mental abilities as we do in Mind Control classes. It will take steady, prolonged, but pleasant application. So far, the exercises I have given you can be practiced alone. In a month or two, when you become proficient, you will be ready for the case work just described. At that point you will need help from others, under carefully controlled conditions. Here is what to do:

Before you even begin the first exercise in this book, form a group of at least six compatible people, who will also learn to practice the exercises. Keep in touch as you progress, and when everyone is ready—when everyone has really mastered the exercises—meet to begin case work. Allow at least an entire day for the first session. Everyone will bring at least four file cards, each with the name, age, and location of a seriously ailing person on one side and the nature of the ailment on the other. Put in plenty of details—these will help when it comes time for verification.

Begin by mentally projecting yourselves into metal. You will not have cubes or cylinders of metals as we have in our classes; you can use dimes and pennies for silver and copper, a ring for gold, a small magnet for iron. You should all examine these objects carefully, then go to your level and imagine one object at a time —picturing it several feet in front of you, above eye level. Imagine the object expanding until it is almost the size of the room, then enter it and perform the various tests.

Do the same with fruits and vegetables, and finally a pet. You can consider these exercises a success when everyone has felt a distinct difference between his examinations of one object and another. It is not necessary that results of each test be clear and detailed, only that the total experience of each object be distinct from the experience of other objects. Your impressions may turn out to be entirely different from someone else's. No matter, the important thing is what you find; that becomes your reference point.

I have not yet developed a way, through the printed page, of helping you evoke counselors. If you are able somehow to do this on your own, fine, but you can proceed perfectly well without them, though your progress may be slower.

For case work, pair off exactly as we do in Mind Control classes. In Chapter 12 you will find the words the orientologist speaks to the psychic as he presents the case. These are exactly the ones we use in class, and I suggest your group use them, too.

I mentioned that you should do this under carefully controlled conditions. Here is what I mean:

1. Select a quiet place where you are unlikely to be interrupted or disturbed.
2. Be sure that every member of the group has practiced all the exercises in this book, in proper order, and has been successful with them.

3. Agree beforehand that there will be no "ego trips." Someone in the group will probably succeed more spectacularly than the rest—at first. This does not mean that he is the "best" or in any sense superior; he has simply succeeded first. Some may not begin to operate psychically until the fifth or sixth meeting, but the slowest often turn out to be the best psychics.

4. If you know a Mind Control graduate, ask him to join you. If he has kept up with his Mind Control, he will be of immense help. If he has let it slip, a brief refresher with this book or another go-around with a Mind Control class (he can do this free of charge) will bring him back.

5. When you are the psychic, set your doubts aside and dive right in. Listen to your hunches—guess—but above all, do not try to reason out your findings. Do not say, "Oh, that can't be" and wait for another impression. What occurs to you on the first thought is more often correct than what occurs on second thought.

Keep talking! Scan the body from top to bottom and describe what you see.

6. When you are the orientologist, do not hint. You want your psychic to succeed, but it will not help if you say, "Go back now to the chest. Sure nothing is wrong there?"

Do not tell the psychic he is wrong. In the early stages, when there may be the greatest number of misses, what often happens is that the psychic picks up other cases rather than the one he is working on. The error is relatively minor and can be corrected with a little practice. Discouraging words from the psychorientologist can bring progress to a halt. Simply say, "I have no information on that."

7. Be patient. If more than a half-million people like you have succeeded, surely you will, too. It may take

you longer working alone and with an informal group, but why rush?

8. Once everyone becomes routinely successful with case work, keep your group together, keep meeting, keep working cases together. You will become better and better at it until one day soon you will be able to work cases alone, becoming more sensitive to the subtle messages of everyday life rather than only to the more powerful ones of serious illness.

9. Do not use anyone who is present as a case. There is a legal distinction between doing this and working on someone who is at a distance. In the first instance it is diagnosis, which must be left to licensed physicians and health caretakers; in the second instance it is psychic detection, which is perfectly all right with the law.

10. When you discover an abnormality in a case you are working, do not rush to give him the news. This is his physician's job. Yours is to develop your psychic abilities so that you can help him and others psychically—and legally. Simply correct mentally what you detect. You detect mentally, so correct mentally.

I warned earlier in this chapter against reading too much meaning into who succeeds first. I learned this lesson in a powerful way when I was teaching one of my earlier classes, in 1967. One of the students was a flight instructor, Jim Needham. Everything was going well for him until the last day of the course. Every case he worked was a hundred-percent miss. No one else in the class of thirty-two did so poorly.

However, Jim saw others doing well, with one direct hit after another. If they could, he could, so he devised his own plan for practicing at home with his wife, who had taken the course with him. She clipped newspaper stories of accident victims, and each night, at level, he would try to work the cases—she giving him their names, ages, sex, and locations, he describing their injuries. Along with this, she read him names from the Yellow Pages and he tried to guess their occupations. Six months of hundred-percent misses, then came a breakthrough; he successfully worked his first case. Then another and still another. He is now with me in Laredo, in charge of training Mind Control instructors, and is one of our most reliable psychics. In fact, Jim can now operate psychically without going to level. It is part of his everyday living.

One evening, at Beta, or outer consciousness, Jim was helping a class through the exercise for evoking counselors. He saw a giant black man, dressed in gold-brocaded robes and wearing a wide, jeweled bracelet, approach one of the students. The student rejected him, and he approached another, then disappeared into his aura.

When the exercise was over, the first student reported that she had only one counselor. Two had appeared, but the male one was Othello; he looked too fearsome. The second student exclaimed, "I got Othello. He didn't come right away, but there he was at the end of the exercise!"

You may not have to persevere as long as Jim Needham did—that is very rare—but if success takes longer to come to you, it does not mean that you have no psychic gift. It means nothing more than that success is taking longer to come to you.

CHAPTER FOURTEEN

HOW TO HELP OTHERS
WITH MIND CONTROL

Detecting illnesses in persons you have never seen is astonishing enough, but we never let it go at that. Into the bodies where we project our awareness we also project healing.

Obviously there is an energy involved in mental projection, an energy aimed by the intentions of our minds. Change these intentions from information gathering to healing and we change what the energy does.

How do we link our intentions to this energy so that it accomplishes what we want? The intention alone, in its pure form, is something like the will. As I said in the chapter on habit control, the will alone is of very little use. Just as we detect abnormalities by visualizing them, we visualize conditions as we want them to be—without the abnormalities. This is psychic healing. It's as simple as that.

For most of the healing that you will want to do, it will not be necessary to master the technique of working cases. You can become an effective psychic healer simply by using your mental screen as you do in problem solving. In fact, even if you are in the early stages of meditation and visualization, you may still achieve some effective results.

Many of life's possibilities hang in a precarious balance. One little push and you can tip this balance your way. Sometimes, of course, the balance is already tipped and it takes a more accomplished psychic—which you will become—to tip it back. If you wait until you are as effective at Mind Control as you would like to be before you begin psychic healing you will waste priceless opportunities to provide needed help.

I began healing work long before I had developed Mind Control, and in fact long before I had an organized methodology for healing. I tried one method after another, with varying results. The important thing is that I did not wait, and a significant number of healings did take place—enough, in fact, that I developed a certain renown as a healer in my area of the U.S.–Mexican border. Many thought I had special gifts or unusual powers; but I had simply read and experimented until I got the hang of it.

One of my early healings shows how different my methods used to be. In 1959 I heard about a parish priest near Laredo who had suffered for fifteen years from a painful swelling of the knees. He was often confined to bed. The pain and confinement were not all that troubled the priest; he was unable to kneel at moments in the celebration of the Mass when kneeling is called for. The Archbishop had granted him a dispensation, but no dispensation could free the poor man from the feeling that he was compromising a sacred ritual.

I went to see him. "I think I can help you," I said. "I am no doctor, but for the past twelve years I have been working on parapsychology and we have obtained results much like those of faith healing, with which you are familiar."

As soon as I said the words "results much like those of faith healing," the priest became more concerned for me than for himself. Parapsychology?

"I have never heard of such a science. I trust you are not getting into anything of which our Holy Church would disapprove."

I explained, as best I could, some of the principles of parapsychology I had learned and how healings can be triggered. Nothing that I said seemed to mesh with this man's theology. He promised to look into it further and perhaps call me sometime soon. The look of compassion on his face and the sound of disbelief in his voice gave me no hope at all that I would hear from him again. I knew, though, that he would pray for my protection from dangers so serious in his mind that they dwarfed even his own plight.

I did hear from the priest a month later and once again sat by his bedside.

"José, as you know, the Lord leads us in strange ways. A few days after your visit I received a circular reviewing a book written by one of the brothers in our order. I found a whole chapter devoted to this parapsychology you were explaining to me the other day. Now I understand this a little better and I am willing to let you try your work on me."

I sat with him for over an hour and spoke of my reading and some of the work I had done. The longer I remained, the more I liked the man. Finally he grew tired and it was time to leave.

"All right then," he said, "when shall we start the treatment?"

"Father, it has already started."

"But I don't understand."

"This thing is mental, Father, and while we were talking I have done the initial work."

I did the rest of the work at home that night. The

next morning the priest was on the telephone and with surprise and joy in his voice reported that a great improvement had taken place during the night.

Three days after my visit he could walk and kneel, and he has never since experienced discomfort in his knees. A miracle? No, a purely natural phenomenon. Here is how I did it.

During the more-than-an-hour chat we were both alert and relaxed, two conditions helpful in healing. The subjects we discussed gave him added confidence in parapsychology. In psychic work, confidence is as important as faith is in religion. Meanwhile I began to visualize him in better health and, just as important, learned to like him more and more. Love is a tremendous power; I wanted that on our side, too.

I did one more thing in preparation for what I would later do that night. To help visualize him later, I studied the priest—his face, the feel of his handshake, his various expressions and mannerisms, the sound of his voice, the overall feeling of being in his presence. This was the "initial work."

Several hours later, when the priest was asleep and I was back home, I did the rest of the job. What I did was totally different from what I do now. I had learned that psychic energies are transferred most effectively when survival is at stake, as I mentioned in the last chapter. Instead of going to my level, as I would today, I held my breath while picturing the priest in perfect health. Long minutes went by, until my body screamed for breath. Still I held on to my image of the priest in perfect health. Meanwhile my brain, in a sort of psychic scream, cried out and the energy of the scream carried the carefully held image of perfect health exactly where it was supposed to go.

Finally I breathed, convinced the job was done, and it was. The method I teach and use today is much easier on the operator and just as effective. Simply learn to use the mental screen vividly, with confidence. Let me outline the procedure for you, step by step.

1. It is helpful, though not necessary, to know the condition of the person you are about to heal. You can learn this psychically or objectively; it does not matter.

2. Go to your meditative level and project this person onto your mental screen as he is, with whatever ailment is troubling him. Place another image on the screen to the left, showing something being done to correct the problem. (If you have not met the person and are not yet ready for case work, try to learn beforehand what he looks like to make your visualization as accurate as possible.)

3. Now project onto the screen—still farther left—a vivid image of the person in perfect health, filled with energy and optimism. In deep meditation you are acutely receptive to what you say to yourself. This particular moment is crucial to developing a conviction that the happy image you now have of the person is the real one —not that it is becoming real or that it will be real, but that it *is* real. The reason for this is that at this meditative level, at Alpha and Theta, your mind is in league with causes; at Beta it deals more with results. By visualizing with conviction in Alpha and Theta you are *causing*. Never mind what you seem to be doing to time by substituting "is" for "will be." Time is something else at this level. Visualize the results you want as being already achieved.

Among the laws of the universe there seems to be a sort of cosmic Bill of Rights which guarantees that all of us, no matter how high or low, no matter how bright or dull, can take part in causing lawful things to happen through the firmness of our desire, belief, and expectancy. This was said earlier, and better, almost 2,000 years ago, as reported by Mark in the New Testament: "What things soever ye desire, when ye pray, believe that ye receive them, and ye shall receive them."

While you visualize this person in perfect health there will come an instant, a very pleasant one, when you know that you have done enough. It is pleasant because it is a feeling of accomplishment. Count yourself out to Beta, one to five, "feeling wide awake and better than before."

The more you practice this technique, the more beautiful coincidences will occur and the more firm will be your belief, which in turn will produce even more beautiful coincidences. As soon as you learn to use your mental screen you can begin to spark this chain reaction.

While the techniques of faith and psychic healing may be different, I believe their principles—and results —are the same. Rituals of faith healing differ from one culture to another, but they have the same twofold effect: to induce a deeper level of mind, and to buttress belief and expectation.

Many healers use methods which exhaust them. They are drained of energy and sometimes lose weight in a single sitting. This is not necessary. In fact, Mind Control methods have the opposite effect. Once we sense that feeling of accomplishment, we experience a lift— not a subtle one; it is quite strong—and we do awaken "feeling better than before." Healing others, we find, is good for the healer.

Many healers believe they cannot heal themselves. Some feel that if they even try this they will lose their "power." We have proved this to be untrue, over and over. Many also believe they must be in the presence of the person they are healing for the "laying on of hands." For those of us who are not licensed physicians or officials of recognized churches, this is illegal. More important in terms of larger laws, it is unnecessary. Absent healing works.

In discussing this in Mind Control classes, we often cite the case of the Centurion's servant whom Christ healed at a distance. Christ did not see the servant, only the Centurion who told Him of the problem. "And his servant was healed in the selfsame hour."

One small observation: Notice that in our folklore, when we make a wish—with a wishbone or when we see a star fall or when we blow out birthday candles—we are admonished not to reveal our wish. This secrecy is probably more than mere child's play; I think there is some wisdom behind it. Keeping our wish—or, more to the point, our visualization of a healing—bottled up in secrecy seems a way to avoid dissipating its energy, maybe even to add to its energy. For this reason, I and many of our lecturers advise students to keep their healing work to themselves. When Christ said after one of His healings, "See that no man know of it," He was not asking for a cover-up; His reasons were deeper.

CHAPTER FIFTEEN

SOME SPECULATIONS

Chapters 3 to 15, which you have just read, were designed, like the Mind Control course, to help you use more of your mind in special ways to solve the kinds of problems that beset every human life. What you have read stems from my more than thirty years of study and experiment. As you can see, I have kept my work on a very practical level, perhaps because I was born very poor and life presented me with practical problems from the beginning.

Along the way, however, it seemed only natural to speculate on the many discoveries that amazed me. Because I have been influenced by a great deal of reading, by learned associates, and perhaps most of all by the very rich tradition of Christianity, I can claim little originality for these thoughts.

One of the things that amazed me was that nothing I discovered to be truly workable conflicted in any way with my religious convictions. For tragic centuries there has been an uncomfortable relationship between science and religion. I have never experienced this personally. What amazed me even more is that my findings did not conflict with any other religion or, in fact, with any established world view. Among our enthusiastic graduates are atheists, Protestants of every denomination,

115

Catholics, Jews, Moslems, Buddhists, and Hindus, along with scientists and scholars of a wide spectrum of disciplines.

Does this mean that there are no values inherent in Mind Control? Are the techniques I developed neither good nor bad, like the multiplication table? I said I would deal with speculations in this chapter, but on this point I have some firm convictions, which I believe I can support with logic. Let me express these in a kind of catechism:

1. Does the universe have laws? Of course—science is discovering them.

2. Can we break these laws? No. We can jump from a building and die, or make ourselves sick, but the laws are not broken; we are.

3. Can the universe think about itself? We know that at least one part of it can: we ourselves. Is it not reasonable to conclude that the whole can?

4. Is the universe indifferent to us? How could it be? We are part of it, and it responds to us.

5. Are we fundamentally good or bad? When we are in closest touch with ourselves—in meditation—we are capable of no harm at all and a vast amount of good.

Were it not for my experiments which prove out number 5, I and my view of reality would be vastly different.

The best definition I ever heard of reality is that it is the one dream we all share. We have only the faintest hints of what it actually is. What we perceive, the way we see things, is largely for our own convenience. Things at a distance are not really smaller, and solid things are not really solid.

Everything is energy. The difference between a color and a sound, between a cosmic ray and a television picture, is frequency, or what energy is doing and how fast. Matter is energy, too, as we learn from $E = MC^2$ —it is energy doing something else, being in another state. An interesting thing about energy—in a world of opposites: up and down, black and white, fast and slow—is that there is no opposite for energy. This is because there is nothing that is not energy, including you and me and everything we think. Thinking both consumes and creates energy, or, to be more accurate, it converts energy.

You can see now why I find little separation between a thought and a thing.

Can thoughts influence things? Of course; energy can.

Can thoughts influence events? Of course; energy can.

Is time energy? I have only the most tentative speculations on this because time presents so many different faces to us. Look at it one way and we think we see it clearly, then look at it another way and it seems altogether different.

To tie our shoelaces or cross a street, we had better think of time as running in a straight line from past through the present into the future. We *must* think of it this way in order to get through the everyday job of living, just as we still conveniently think of the sun as rising and setting, as if the old astronomy of Copernicus had never been proved wrong. From this perspective we can remember the past, experience the present, and look uncertainly, if at all, into the future.

Not so from another perspective. In Alpha and Theta we can look into the future as well as the past. Coming events *do* cast their shadows before, and we can be trained to see them. This ability is known by the now-respectable word "precognition." It was far less respectable when I won the Mexican lottery.

If in Alpha and Theta the future can be seen here and now, it must send ahead some kind of energy, which we can tune in to. For time to send any kind of energy anywhere, it must be an energy itself.

I discovered something rather strange about how we perceive time many years ago when I was experimenting with hypnosis. When I put two of my children through age regression—taking them back in time— if the change of scenery from present to past started too abruptly, they would lurch to their right just as when we are moving forward on a bus and it stops abruptly, we lurch forward.

The children felt that in traveling backward in time they were traveling to their right. When I returned them to the present and stopped, the reverse would happen; they would lurch to the left. Many of my early experiments with different subjects confirmed this.

Later, when I abandoned hypnosis for controlled meditation, I wanted to learn how, subjectively, to move backward and forward in time. I faced east because Oriental disciplines specify facing in that direction and east seemed as good a direction as any. Then I wondered if I would be able to move around more freely in time if, taking a cue from the hypnosis experiments, I put the future on my left and the past on my right.

On this planet the sun brings the new day from the east and carries it to the west. If I faced south during meditation, east would be on my left and west on my right and I would thus be oriented to the planetary flow of time.

Whether or not I really discovered the direction in which time flows on earth, I do not know; I do know that once I began facing south I felt better oriented in time and could move around in it more easily.

* * *

Now let us deal with a larger question. I have mentioned Higher Intelligence a number of times in past chapters. Is this some noncommittal way of mine of referring to God? I cannot prove what I am about to say; I must speak from faith. My answer is no, by Higher Intelligence I do not mean God. I use capitals for the words because I am so respectful of it, but to me it is not God.

The universe seems to do what it does with remarkable efficiency—without a scrap of waste. When I put one foot in front of another, I cannot believe it is one of God's preoccupations to see that I do not trip, nor, for that matter, is it a concern of Higher Intelligence; it is mine. I was genetically programmed to learn to walk; that was God's work. Now that I have learned, the routine steps are up to me.

However, some steps in life are not routine, and I may need information not available through the five senses to make a decision. For this I turn to Higher Intelligence. Sometimes I need overall advice of transcending importance. For this I turn to God. I pray.

I see various levels of intelligence as a continuum, going from inanimate matter to the vegetable to the animal, then to the human and to Higher Intelligence and finally to God. I believe I have scientifically found ways of communicating with each level, from the inanimate to Higher Intelligence. I have conducted experiments under controlled conditions and proved them out through repetition, and anyone who follows the instructions in this book or takes the course in Mind Control can reproduce them. This is what I mean by "scientific." Much of the rest is speculation and faith; not this.

Just one more of my speculations: In the perspective of our long history, we humans have just recently completed an evolutionary stage. This was the development of our brain. This is now over with and done; we have all the brain cells we are going to get. The next stage is already in progress: the development of our mind. Soon what are now considered special psychic abilities will be commonplace for all of us, as they are today among Mind Control graduates and those readers who follow the steps I have outlined in this book.

You can see from these speculations that I have a certain view of the world and of what constitutes truth and reality. Now it is fair for you to ask, "Do Mind Control graduates emerge from their experiences with views similar to these?" No, far from it. Let me give you an example.

Among those who remain closest to Mind Control practices, an amazing number become vegetarians. Harry McKnight, who works closest with me, did this recently. I enjoy a good steak.

CHAPTER SIXTEEN

A CHECKLIST

Once you have mastered all the techniques I have outlined—if you are like most Mind Control graduates—you may use a few that work best for you and let the others slip. You can easily recapture the knack and the good results with a quick review of those you may have neglected.

To save you time, here is a list of all the techniques described in Chapters 3 through 14:

CHAPTER SEVENTEEN

A PSYCHIATRIST WORKS
WITH MIND CONTROL

In the past several chapters José explained Mind Control and gave detailed instructions on how you can put much of it to work. You can see that very deep levels of consciousness are involved in Mind Control, and you may wonder, as others have, whether you face any dangers as you explore, perhaps for the first time, the powerful depths of your own mind.

José and those close to him in directing the Mind Control organization say that experience so far shows that the benefits of the training are not in even the smallest way offset by any "untoward side effects," to use a medical phrase. Putting it another way, no one who has taken the course is any the worse for it, as far as José and his colleagues know.

One Mind Control graduate, a member of the medical profession, has put Mind Control's safety to an acid test. He is Dr. Clancy D. McKenzie, a prominent Philadelphia psychiatrist and psychoanalyst, director of the Philadelphia Psychiatric Consultation Service, member of the staff of The Philadelphia Psychiatric Center, and in active private practice. He is also a long-time student of Yoga and other meditational disciplines, biofeedback, and parapsychology.

As part of his studies in these fields, he enrolled in the Mind Control course in 1970. "I wanted to see if they were actually teaching clairvoyance, as a number of my patients who had benefited from the course reported to me. I became convinced that something psychic was taking place, and I have since devoted a good deal of time and thought to investigating it further."

Two other things sparked his interest in Mind Control: a comment made by Sigmund Freud toward the end of his career, and something that happened in a Mind Control class.

Freud had said that the most promising direction for psychotherapy to take in the future is toward mobilization of the patient's energies. Dr. McKenzie clearly saw people in the Mind Control class using energies they never knew they had.

But he saw something else in this class: "Three persons out of the thirty were emotionally disturbed and there was a fourth whose stability was in question. What was the reason? Did the course precipitate emotional illness or had they been ill when they arrived? Were my own disturbed patients who had benefited from the course merely lucky?"

The most practical way to find out, he reasoned, was to test people before and after the course. The test would be to observe closely those who were the most psychologically vulnerable. He and a colleague, Dr. Lance S. Wright, professor of psychiatry at the University of Pennsylvania, launched a study. During the following four and a half years 189 psychiatric patients volunteered to go through Mind Control training. To make the test still more stringent, they focused an even more detailed study on those in this group who were psychotic, borderline psychotic, or who had recovered from psychosis. There were 75 of these.

From their observations of the beneficial effect of the course on healthy people, the results of these tests were no surprise to Dr. McKenzie and Dr. Wright. There was consistent improvement in mental health among the psychiatric patients.

For those interested in the close reasoning and tight controls that guide scientific studies, here are some details. Of the 75 patients in the disturbed group, 66 were from Dr. McKenzie's practice. They represented 100 percent of his psychotic and borderline psychotic patients who were willing to take the course.

At the outset of the study, patients were sent cautiously one at a time so they could be monitored closely for any ill effects, on themselves or the class. Also, they were sent during what Dr. McKenzie describes as "their more stable periods." Later he found he could send patients during their less stable periods; four went while they were actively delusional. Still later he felt comfortable sending several disturbed patients at a time, sometimes six or more.

As part of his study, he tested 58 of these patients before and after the course to see what changes it might cause. The test, the Experiential World Inventory, consists of 400 questions designed to measure a person's perception of reality—something like the famous Rorschach ink-blot test, but in written form. The difference between the before and after scores was impressive: 36 showed dramatic improvement in reality perception, 21 remained about the same, and 1 showed a drop.

The person whose score dropped was a twenty-nine-year-old catatonic schizophrenic who—for the first time in his life—stopped taking medication and began dating. "Clinically," observed Dr. McKenzie, "he had more emotional energy and a brighter outlook following the training. However, the dating threw him into conflict and he became disturbed two weeks after the course. He did not require hospitalization."

All these patients, of course, had been in psychotherapy—many for a year or more—which gave Dr. McKenzie an excellent opportunity to see what actual clinical changes had taken place after the course. Here are some of his findings:

One patient, a thirty-year-old schizophrenic, earlier in his life had believed he was under orders, sent telepathically, to kill someone. Fortunately he could never find the right person. During therapy sessions after the course he was able to discuss his "delusional system" for the first time. His emotional energy was much greater, and he had a brighter outlook on life. Soon he returned to school to earn a Ph.D. "His ability to do so was directly related to his taking the course," explains Dr. McKenzie.

Of twenty-eight patients suffering from various types of depression (involutional, psychotic, schizo-affective, and manic-depressive), 26 felt pleasantly better after the course. The other two, who reported feeling more depressed, not only scored better on the questionnaire but, like the others, were able to work through problems they had been unable to deal with before.

A twenty-one-year-old woman was determined to commit suicide and was in the early stage of acute psychosis. She assured Dr. McKenzie that nothing he could do would help; she would commit suicide anyway. He recommended that she take the course. By the end of the week he was "absolutely amazed; she responded better than any of the other patients had. It was one of the most dramatic remissions I had ever seen."

She found a new calm, was more rational, and her thoughts no longer raced in quickly changing directions. Just as important, most of her burden of pessimism was lifted. In a clinical report, Drs. McKenzie and Wright say, "Hospitalization and high doses of medication could not have calmed her as much. She repeated the course two weeks later and again there was improvement. The changes were dramatic; she was better able to work in therapy over the next six months." A year later, Dr. McKenzie found her fully recovered from her acute illness.

Psychoses, of course, are severe mental disorders. Neuroses are far less severe. Of the 189 patients who took Mind Control, 114 were suffering only from neurosis. All of these benefited too.

Summarizing their clinical findings in the aforementioned paper, the doctors wrote:

> Those who continued to practice Mind Control after the training were able greatly to alter their lives by it, and even those who did not practice it were able to use it in times of crisis, when they had to cope with stress or had important decisions to make. For everyone it seemed to be a mind expansion experience, a revelation that they could use their mind in other ways. Group enthusiasm mounted toward the end of the course and most persons experienced a higher emotional energy.
>
> The disturbed group also showed an impressive change clinically. Only the one mentioned [the twenty-nine-year-old who had just begun dating] became more upset, and the others at least derived some benefit from the training. Many persons with flat affect [little or no emotional response] showed enthusiasm about something for the first time. There did seem to be a change in emotional energy after the course and an improvement in affect. They had a more positive outlook about their

future, and for some there was a better understanding of their psychotic processes. The delusional patients were clearly less delusional after the training.

There was a greater relaxation and lessening of anxiety. Patients learned to rely on their own resources to understand, cope with and solve problems, and to be able to do so gave them more confidence.

With all but one of the 189 patients benefiting from the course, Dr. McKenzie concludes that it is "more than just safe and beneficial; it can be immensely useful as an integral part of psychotherapy." He now has almost all his patients take the course. Some of them shorten the length of their therapy by as much as two years with Mind Control techniques.

One of these techniques, Dream Control, he says "may very well prove to be a major breakthrough in psychiatry. It is a swift and reliable way to understand and solve problems."

Trained in Freudian analysis, Dr. McKenzie sees no conflict between the way Freudians interpret spontaneous dreams and the way Mind Control graduates interpret their programmed dreams. "The Freudian dream wish becomes the wish to have the answer," he explains. However, he cautions, "It is necessary to make certain an unconscious dream wish did not supersede the conscious wish to have the answer."

A patient whom Dr. McKenzie had been treating for some time called to say she was about to be admitted to a hospital because of chest and stomach pains. He told her he wanted her in a psychiatric hospital instead. The call was no surprise; he had seen this coming for some time. Her mental condition had been worsening.

In the psychiatric hospital, Dr. McKenzie told her to

program a dream to answer four questions: What is the problem? Where is it? What caused it? How can I get rid of it?

Here is what she dreamed: She, her husband, and their three children were driving along a winding road. It began to snow and the car slid off the road. Soon the car was covered with snow. Her husband told her to cut off the engine; then eight or ten people came from the city to dig them out. When they emerged from the car, their three children were gone.

Just ahead, the road came to a dead end. Another road went off at a right angle into another road at a right angle, which in turn led to still another road—a superhighway, also at a right angle.

As he heard her recount this dream, Dr. McKenzie suspected she was describing an intestinal tract and asked her to draw a map of the "winding road." She did and, sure enough, the road accurately followed the course of a human intestinal tract—all in correct proportion. What's more, a later medical examination found an obstruction at a spot corresponding exactly with where her car slid from the road—where the small intestine meets the large one. In other words, this woman's dream (she knew almost nothing about anatomy; she is a high-school drop-out) accurately pinpointed her obstruction in a one-inch segment of a twenty-foot human intestinal tract!

Still more: The snow, according to the symbolism of her dream, was a dairy product which caused her intestinal upset and in some way triggered the build-up of the obstruction.

Her husband's advice to cut off the engine was—again, in symbolic form—the best advice she could get: It meant "shut off the fuel supply to the body; stop eating."

The eight or ten persons who dug them out are, in

dream language, the fingers of the two hands. This may represent the healing "laying on of hands" or surgery. The sudden absence of the children was wish fulfillment. She wanted them out of the way to get more of her husband's attention for herself.

Dr. McKenzie had her transferred to a medical hospital because, normally, an intestinal obstruction like this calls for immediate surgery. However—armed with this understanding of her dream and with the knowledge, gained in Mind Control class, of the power of the mind over the body, plus the anticipation of surgery—she began to release the obstruction. An hour after Dr. McKenzie's dream-based diagnosis was medically confirmed at the hospital, she had freed herself of the obstruction and no surgery was necessary. Her surgeon was amazed.

Dr. McKenzie later learned that this woman had had surgery for an intestinal obstruction four times in the past twenty years, and her surgeons told him that each time it had been in the same place. It appeared she had learned to produce the illness whenever there was a psychological need for it.

Later, this woman's eighteen-year-old daughter came to him with a problem—she was pregnant and unmarried. "What on earth should I do?" she asked. Once again he advised Dream Control to find the answer. In her dream, a man appeared. He said, "Have the baby, wait three years, marry the man, then move out of the state."

"I couldn't have given her better advice," Dr. McKenzie said. "The divorce rate among teenagers is eighty percent, so three years' waiting at home was logical. The man was the right person for her, but for a successful marriage they would be better off away from home, far from parents."

In another case, Dream Control led to a totally new

therapeutic technique, which saved years of therapy time. This patient's problem was that whenever her husband was more than ten minutes late for dinner she slashed her wrists. For months Dr. McKenzie tried to explain that, while she *thought* she was responding to her husband's tardiness, she was actually experiencing an earlier feeling, from childhood, when her alcoholic father would not come home. Once she understood this she would stop her wrist-slashing, but Dr. McKenzie was not getting through. The way things were going, the woman faced two more years of twice-a-week therapy. Dr. McKenzie suggested that she program a dream.

Her dream turned out to be an amazingly creative one, which solved her problem overnight.

She dreamed that Dr. McKenzie taped some statements that upset her the most. She played this tape at home and recorded her reactions to it on a second tape. Then she played the second tape for Dr. McKenzie to interpret. To each of his interpretations she exclaimed, "Oh, how stupid of me!" His interpretations pointed out that she was confusing two different realities, past and present. Her dream led her to understand this for the first time. She never slashed her wrists again.

"This remarkable programmed dream cured the patient altogether. A three-year follow-up confirmed that she remained well," Dr. McKenzie reported.

Another patient suffered from claustrophobia, and he struggled for more than a year to get at its cause. It turned out to be an interesting one. In a programmed dream he and three other persons were in a rectangle outlined by a rope on the ground. Outside this rectangle, at one corner, was a smaller one, also outlined by a rope. Everyone was trying to get out of the larger rectangle through the smaller one.

The significance of this dream becomes clear when you see the larger area as the womb, the smaller one as the cervix. Outside was a green pasture with cows (breasts).

One of the patient's companions ran toward the smaller rectangle but was stopped by an invisible barrier (the uterine wall). A string of tin cans was attached to him near his belt buckle (an umbilical cord).

The patient knew that somehow he would have to get out of there, but he decided to let the others go first. It gave him a sort of nervous feeling, like giving a speech—something he knew he had to do even though it caused stress and anxiety (birth trauma)—but there was relief after it was over.

The other three in the rectangle were his brothers and sister.

This one dream gave him the insight he needed into his claustrophobia.

What makes the dream particularly interesting is not that it takes a person back prior to birth—this is fairly common—but its reference to the "invisible barrier." Does this, Dr. McKenzie wonders, suggest the possibility of clairvoyance prior to birth?

Dr. McKenzie not only advises his patients to use Mind Control, he uses it himself to help his patients. "Some of the most amazing wisdom comes to me when I'm using Dream Control."

One night he programmed a dream about a patient in psychoanalysis, a twenty-seven-year-old man who had not dated in two years. Women were against him, "and besides, they were no good." In his dream, Dr. McKenzie heard himself say, "It's okay with me if you never have a heterosexual relationship." Next time the patient complained about women, that is exactly what Dr. McKenzie said to him.

It worked. The patient was stunned. Avoiding women was his way of resisting treatment—now it would no longer work. Besides, he was panicked when he thought of never having a healthy relationship with a woman.

That night he did.

Dr. McKenzie, who has become a consultant to Silva Mind Control, continues to search for new ways to use Mind Control to improve and speed up psychiatric treatment. At the same time, he is looking for ways to use Mind Control in far broader areas of medical practice—in the diagnosis of illnesses.

The first step in this search is to find ways of measuring the reliability of Mind Control's technique of working cases. After three years of research, he believes he is coming close to what he terms an "absolute research design," one that eliminates all the variables and measures only what it sets out to measure. His purpose is to find ways to put case working to medical use.

Medical diagnosis sometimes involves exploratory surgery or drugs that may cause discomfort or danger to the patient—and no diagnostic technique is accurate all the time. Psychic diagnosis would pose no hazard for the patient, provided its reliability can be demonstrated. This is what Dr. McKenzie is working on.

The first time he tried his new research design was in a Mind Control graduate class of 30 persons. The accuracy of the results was greater than what chance would produce by 200 to one. He was encouraged, but he wanted to refine his methods even more and to arrange for the scoring to be computerized.

He checked out his plans with the statistics department of the University of Pennsylvania, and they agreed that he had indeed eliminated the variables that plague psychic research and that his measurements would be accurate.

The Mind Control newsletter published drawings of two human bodies (see pages 134–35) with circles for readers to check. They were given, as in case work, the

IMPORTANT: The purpose of this experiment is to correctly detect the location of the abnormality or illness. *Please limit your activities to **detection** so as not to affect the illness during the experiment.*

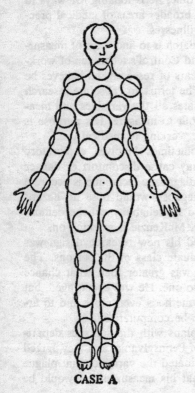

CASE A

Instructions:

1. Debbie Veccio is 23 years old and lives in Miami, Florida. She has a medical problem that you may be able to help. Please go to your Mind Control level and picture or imagine Debbie, with a desire on your part to locate her illness. When you think you have located her illness, fill in ONE circle only on diagram A, nearest where you sensed or guessed it to be.

Important: If you fill in more than one circle per diagram, your answer will be disqualified.

Allow at least 10 minutes to elapse before going on to case B.

2. Cynthia Cohen is 21 years old and lives in Miami, Florida. She has a medical problem that you may be able to help. Please go to your Mind Control level and picture or imagine Cynthia, with a desire on your part to locate her illness. When you think you have located her illness, fill in ONE circle only in diagram B, nearest where you sensed or guessed it to be. Because the nature of this experiment involves detection only, do not send corrective healing until . . .

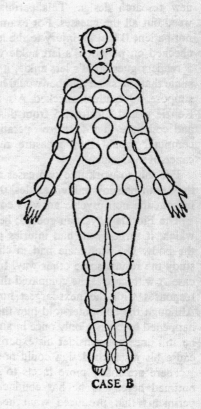

CASE B

name, age, sex, and location of two persons who were ill. What they were not given, what Dr. McKenzie himself did not know, was the nature of the illnesses. The Florida physician who gave him the cases was to reveal this only after results were in.

Doing two cases rather than one is central to the new research design. This permits Dr. McKenzie to weed out all the guesses. For example, if patient A but not patient B had an injury to the left ankle, any circles checked on patient B's left ankle would be guesses. If 5 readers guessed B's left ankle, it is reasonable to assume that the same number would be guessing A's. Now suppose 50 readers checked A's left ankle. Dr. McKenzie would substract 5 from this number as guesses and conclude that 45 were operating psychically. The computer would then measure the statistical significance of the results.

For this to work, the two cases must be different. If they both had injured left ankles, this method of weeding out the non-psychic answers could not be used.

The Florida physician goofed; he supplied two cases which, it turned out, had injuries to the same area of the body. Dr. McKenzie had to change his plans and study the results some other way. Instead of comparing case A with case B, he compared the number of correct responses with the next-largest number of responses. Although the computer told him the results could have happened by chance only once in almost a billion times, he still does not consider his experiment conclusive because his research design could not be followed.

There are many more facets to his design than are outlined here, and he has conducted many other experiments that produced what he terms "statistically significant results." His entire project is so significant that we will surely hear more about it when he has refined his technique even more. Instead of simply having them check a circle to indicate the location of an illness, he will give Mind Control graduates lists of medical ailments to check, thereby providing specific diagnosis.

"These preliminary studies," he said, "point toward high levels of statistical significance. I am not ready, though, to draw conclusions from them. A lot more painstaking work is needed. If later studies are equally encouraging, we may have a way of putting psychics to work to help physicians in their diagnosis in ways even more reliable than those being used now. This just could turn out to be a medical breakthrough. It's too early to say for sure, but that's what I'm working toward."

Mind Control's Research Director, J. Wilfred Hahn, a biochemist and former president of Mind Science Foundation, shares Dr. McKenzie's hopes. "Ever since the nineteenth century, when the scientific method was brought to bear on psychic research, uncontrolled (sometimes unknown) variables left questions hanging over the findings. Whether Dr. McKenzie achieves a medical breakthrough is, as he says, yet to be determined. But I believe he has already achieved a breakthrough in his research method. From all the data he gathers, he can concentrate the psychic responses—he can eliminate all the garbage, leaving only what he wants to study, just as a chemist studying a single trace element in water can eliminate the water and all other elements except the one he wants to study."

CHAPTER EIGHTEEN

YOUR SELF-ESTEEM WILL SOAR

"We waste too much of our time dragging ourselves under. If we spent one half of it just researching in our mind how to deal with life, we'd find we're so much stronger than we think," singer-actress Carol Lawrence was quoted as saying in the *Chicago Tribune*, November 14, 1975. She became a Mind Control graduate on the recommendation of another graduate, singer Marguerite Piazza.

True, most of us are imprisoned by narrow ideas of who we are and what we can do. You will soon experience the exhilaration of smashing these confines and finding new freedoms outside them. When you see what you are capable of, your self-esteem will soar. A number of studies have been made of this, and the results are in. They cover large groups with no special problems as well as others whose self-esteem is obviously in shambles—students as well as alcoholics, drug addicts, prisoners, and the welfare poor.

Let us look first at students. Mind Control has been taught, often as a full-credit course, in twenty-four colleges and universities, sixteen high schools, and eight elementary schools.

You might expect that the same course taught the same way in different schools to students of different ages and different cultural and economic backgrounds would achieve different results. Not so—the results have been so uniform that it can now be safely claimed that in basic respects they are predictable. Introduce Mind Control in a school and the result will be students with more powerful self-direction, greater self-guidance stemming from improved ability to solve problems on their own. In other words, greater ego strength. This has been scientifically measured by Dr. George De Sau, former Director of Educational Research for Silva Mind Control and previously Director of Counseling and Testing at the Williamsport (Pennsylvania) Area Community College.

The first test, in 1972, was at Hallahan High School in Philadelphia, where 2,000 students took the course. A week before and two weeks after, 220 randomly selected students were given the High School Personality Questionnaire,* which consists of some 140 questions that sensitively measure a person's self-image. His total self-image can then be drawn up as a sort of portrait with fourteen characteristics—adventurous, zestful, self-assured, and so on. The test is widely used in research and counseling.

The self-image portraits of these 220 students were combined into a single group profile, then compared before and after. Results: major shifts toward higher ego strength, self-assurance, and composure, and away from impatience, insecurity, and detachment. In some respects students remained unchanged—as in balance between dominance and submissiveness, tender- and tough-mindedness. What all this added up to was that these students had greater respect for themselves after Mind Control than they had before.

Naturally, with life's changing patterns, our view of

* Published by the Institute for Personality and Ability Testing.

ourselves changes from day to day. If we gave the test to a randomly selected group and then repeated it three weeks later, we would find some changes. This too has been studied by those who developed the test. The random changes that would occur by chance are a normal expectation, and their rate has been calculated. To evaluate the results at Hallahan High, it was necessary to determine by how much the reported changes exceeded those that chance alone could produce. Here is what was found:

For chance to produce positive changes in ego strength as great as those brought about by Mind Control at Hallahan High, the test would have to be given more than a thousand times to a randomly selected group—more than a thousand times to match the change in self-assurance, more than a thousand times to match the change in composure. What made the difference was not chance but Mind Control.

While the course was in progress, a *Philadelphia Daily News* reporter, Joe Clark, interviewed some students during a lunch break. In an article that appeared September 27, 1972, he quoted thirteen-year-old Kathy Brady, who had been biting her nails since she was eight: "I always bit them when I got nervous. When I was in the auditorium this morning I felt like biting them, but I didn't. I just thought to myself, 'Don't bite your nails.' I closed my eyes and relaxed."

Pat Eisenlohr told him she had passed up a fight with her younger brother, something that had hardly ever happened before. "I told myself, 'There's no use in getting mad. Why fight?' I didn't. I also got rid of a headache this morning by telling myself to get rid of it. I know it sounds weird, but it works."

Now let's compare results at this school with two other studies, one at Lawrenceville, a co-ed Catholic high school in Pittsburgh, and the other at St. Fidelis, a Catholic high school for men planning to become priests.

At Lawrenceville and St. Fidelis, as at Hallahan, the greatest change among the students was in ego strength. What's more, this change was uniform—in each school the group profile improved to a degree that could have occurred by chance alone only once in a thousand times. The same degree of change occurred in composure at Hallahan and Lawrenceville, though less at St. Fidelis. Varying degrees of change in self-assurance, though all sharply positive, occurred at all three schools.

The findings of which the above are a part did not fully satisfy Dr. De Sau. Although he was cheered by the positive results and reassured by the uniform pattern of benefits from Mind Control, something was missing. Tests of a group before, then two weeks after Mind Control training do not indicate whether these benefits are of lasting value. Testing four months after the training would.

Dr. De Sau did this at Lawrenceville and St. Fidelis; he faced some surprises. In all the above characteristics —ego strength, self-assurance, composure—the students of both schools improved far more over the four-month period than they had during the two weeks immediately following the course!

In his report on these studies, Dr. De Sau concluded:

> Perhaps the changes which took place with the above students in their various educational settings can best be evaluated from a perspective such as that held by John Holt, educator and author. It is Holt's position that the educational process has often been one of teaching stupidity through contributing to the increasing of anxiety, guilt, and

almost continuous reliance upon the external environment for approval or disapproval—all the conditions which may produce conforming, neurotic, robopathic behavior but do little to enhance education or human growth. There are reasonable grounds to believe the same conditions are found in other societal institutions.

The research data above indicate, at least from the educational perspective, a refreshing, viable alternative. A factor of change which is persistent and strong after Mind Control training is that of a shifting to internal points of reference—another way of saying the recognition by an individual of his own value and a significant step toward self-control as opposed to being controlled by external *others*.

In most schools where Mind Control is taught, teachers are urged to take it, too. The reasons—all except one—are obvious enough, considering the benefits of the training. The teachers become less flappable, more patient, far easier for students to spend their class hours with.

It is well known that a teacher who expects less from students gets less, and one who expects more gets more. The teacher trained in Mind Control has had firsthand experience with what in Chapter 14 José calls the "cosmic Bill of Rights," with its humanity-wide jurisdiction. No teacher with this training can ever again scoff at anyone's "mental equipment"—he knows the vast scope of every human mind too well for that. He is a better teacher as a result, even if his students have never heard of Mind Control.

However, when the students and the teacher are Mind Control graduates, great things happen in the classroom.

One grade-school teacher in Buffalo teaches her students to "tune in" to George Washington and other figures of the past to help them study history, using techniques they learned in the final hours of Mind Control, when they worked cases. This way they experience history. And to help them later, when they take tests, they tune in to her and find confirmation of their answers.

Another teacher, this one on the college level, has her students tune in to philosophers for explanations of points they find obscure in their writings. "It works!" she says.

Mrs. Joe Lytle, a Mind Control lecturer in Virginia Beach, takes special delight in teaching youngsters from ages seven to seventeen. Some of her experiences were reported in the *Ledger-Star* of Norfolk (July 16, 1975) under the headline "Students Excel After Course in Mind Control." One of her students was on medication for hyperkinesis. The mother of this overactive youngster is quoted as saying, "The changes were absolutely fantastic after the course. My son was able to stop taking the medicine and his grades went from C's to A's. Mind Control gave him the knowledge that he had the power to change."

Another student's grades in junior high school jumped from C's before the course to A's after it. Still another was failing her spelling tests. After the course she made A's on all her spelling tests, and in one year her reading ability jumped from fourth- to ninth-grade level.

There was no practical way to compare those who chose to take the course with those who did not, or to measure the difference between the two groups afterward, because at the three high schools where Dr. De Sau conducted the before and after tests virtually all the students signed up for Mind Control.

This opportunity came, however, at the University of Scranton, in Scranton, Pennsylvania. Professor Donald L. Angell of the Department of Human Resources offered the course to graduate students in Rehabilitation Counseling. Enough students decided not to take the course to permit him and Dr. De Sau to study some differences. They gave a test similar to the one used at the high schools—though designed for adults—to 35 students who took the course and 35 who did not.

Differences between the two groups showed up even before the course. Those who elected to take it were, according to test results, more open to experience and more inner-directed. Those who did not want the course were more traditional, rule-bound, and practical.

A month after the course, the two groups were tested again and, while the original differences remained, other significant ones had cropped up: The Mind Control group was more emotionally stable and mature, more self-assured, more relaxed than the other.

In short, this study suggests that those who choose to take Mind Control are different from those who do not, and that once they take it they benefit.

While a boost to self-esteem is important to everyone, it can be of life-saving importance to the drug addict fighting his way to freedom from this addiction. Mind Control has limited experience with drug addicts, but the experience has proved instructive.

Paul Grivas, co-director of the Mind Control Center in Manhattan, wanted to see what Mind Control could do for the addicted. He volunteered to start with four addicts, two of them on methadone, two still on heroin. The two on methadone found the course useful, but it did not free them from methadone. Methadone is highly addictive and is used in many drug programs to free the addicts from heroin. To withdraw from methadone is physically painful and the pains, these addicts said, were so severe that they could not concentrate on their Mind Control exercises.

One of the addicts still on heroin faced a family crisis the first day of the course and dropped out. The remaining one was able to detoxify himself—to become free of the drug for several months after the course. Then he telephoned Mr. Grivas to report that he was back on heroin. He asked to repeat the course. Mr. Grivas spent a day with him to reinforce his Mind Control training, and again he became free of the drug. Months later he was still free; then he moved away and Mr. Grivas lost touch with him.

The second effort to help addicts through Mind Control was at a community project in the Bronx, with eighteen former addicts, some of whom were administrators and staff of the project itself. Those who took the course said they felt far more in control of themselves than ever before, and several of them, months later, reported they were even able to pass on some of their training to their families. Reliable testing before and after was not possible because three months later many of the original eighteen were no longer available.

Has anything been learned from these two experiences? Yes, says Paul Grivas. While there is not yet statistical proof, his experience indicates two things:

First, Mind Control should not enter an addict's life for forty-eight hours and then leave the rest up to him. For most of us it is a permanently transforming experience, but for the addict, with years, perhaps a lifetime, of strong negative conditioning to overcome, plus a mental *and* physical addiction, a greatly extended period of frequent reinforcement is necessary. "Give me a drug rehabilitation program where I can do this," Grivas says, "and I'm sure I'll get results."

Second, difficult as drug addiction is to overcome,

the addict takes more easily to Mind Control training than do many others. The reason, Mr. Grivas believes, is that Mind Control involves an altered state of consciousness. While most people have never altered their consciousness, the drug addict has done it often. What he has not done before is enter a useful level of mind where he *gains* control instead of losing it. This is where Mind Control holds special promise for the addict.

Although there have been no extensive studies in this area, there are frequent enough success stories from individual graduates to suggest that Mr. Grivas' confidence in Mind Control is well founded.

Here is one from a graduate who cured his own addiction in 1971. He is still "clean."

I knew I had a serious problem: an addiction to heroin. How a course called Mind Control, which claimed among other things to help people eliminate undesired habits, was going to help me when I had already tried most drug rehabilitation methods was beyond my present level of understanding. Skeptical as I was, after going to psychiatrists, psychotherapists, methadone programs, and hospitals, I was willing to try anything! I was convinced I would not stay alive the three more years to my thirtieth birthday unless I stopped heroin use and the lifestyle it required to obtain up to $200 a day worth of drugs.

"A habit is nothing more than impressions on brain cells that have been reinforced by repetition," said the Mind Control instructor. "Change the programming at the cause level, the subconscious mind," he continued, "and you change the behavior patterns at the effect level, the outer conscious dimension." It made sense to me logically but my emotional levels were telling me I needed to use drugs to desensitize myself to life and the negative feelings I had about myself. Then the instructor gave us a technique for changing our self-image from a weak, no-willpower, ineffective person to a confident, self-reliant, healthy-self-imaged human being.

Still skeptical, but with a glimmer of hope, I began to change myself in my imagination at the "Alpha" level. I programmed myself three times a day, morning, noon, and night, that by July 20, which was thirty days from the date of my initial programming, all desire for drugs would disappear forever. During the thirty days, I continued to use drugs but decreased the amount used slowly, planning it so that I would be off drugs completely by my target date.

On that great day in July I stopped using drugs and have never used them since. It was not at all like the many times before, when I would stop using drugs only to return a few days or weeks later. This time my "gut" feeling was I genuinely had no desire for drugs. No willpower, no substitutions, no suppressing of feelings and desires. It worked! Free at last!

Alcoholism, another addiction, is far more widespread than drug addiction and darkens many more lives—millions of them in the U.S. alone. Its victims also have a desperate need to overcome feelings of helplessness, failure, and guilt, to build self-confidence and composure to ease their return to health.

These needs were met when 15 alcoholics took Mind Control in 1973 as part of a research project at a halfway house where they were under treatment. The results were measured by Dr. De Sau. He administered the same personality test he had used earlier with the graduate students at the University of Scranton and, as in the earlier study, he gave it once immediately before and again a month after the course.

The sharpest contrast between these 15 persons before the course and after it was in manipulative behavior. There was a shift in the group profile away from sly control of events toward greater candor and openness in the pursuit of goals, a shift which chance would produce only one time in a hundred times. Other changes generally followed the pattern seen among the high-school and graduate students described earlier. They had greater ego strength and self-assurance, were more relaxed and open to new experiences—all qualities of priceless value to anyone struggling for freedom from alcohol.

One of the most significant changes was a reduction in "threat sensitivity," or anxiety. Dr. De Sau wrote, "The area of threat sensitivity, with its high autonomic tenseness and overactivity, may be of considerable importance in understanding the behavior of the alcoholic. It is very possible that alcoholics use alcohol as a means of attempting to balance out their mental/physical symptoms. Alcohol as a response to balance the mind/body in a threat situation could provide relief from that anxiety level. An improved self-concept and ability to handle anxiety would seem to be a meaningful alternative to alcohol."

The director of the halfway house reported how each of the 15 new Mind Control graduates was doing six months later. (To preserve their privacy, they are simply referred to as "subject," or "S," rather than by name.)

Subject 1: No relapse since undergoing a 90-day rehabilitation program. S since taking the Mind Control course has progressed from a very passive, withdrawn individual to an affable, outgoing, and dry-witted humorist.

Subject 2: Since taking Mind Control, S has not experienced any relapses and has left the residency and treatment program at the halfway house. It seems that S is developing a sense of well-being and confidence in self.

Subject 3: No relapses since undergoing rehabilitation treatment in hospital program. Since the Mind Control course S has experienced definite progress in A.A. program.

Subject 4: No relapses since hospitalization prior to taking Mind Control. The Mind Control course has very definitely reinforced his therapeutic treatment program.

Subject 5: No relapse has been experienced by S since discharge from hospital rehabilitation program.

Subject 6: No relapses. The S's sense of well-being is very definitely improving. Improvement is reflected in an apparent stabilization of his entire family. His grades in college have also improved.

Subject 7: To date S has not experienced any relapses. After Mind Control course, S discontinued A.A. program. However, it is evident that he is living the A.A. philosophy. Family relations are also seemingly improving.

Subject 8: No relapses since taking the Mind Control course. Family relations have vastly improved. S has changed from a caustic, angry type of individual to an affable "Love thy neighbor" temperament.

Subject 9: The subject, a female, has had no relapses and is presently employed.

Subject 10: No relapse. S is now goal-oriented and has definitely altered self-imposed limitations and is looking for opportunities for higher achievement.

Subject 11: Since taking Mind Control, S has stated

his life has progressively become better, which is evident in the sense of well-being exhibited by his family and in his work record. No relapses have been experienced by S.

Subject 12: Twelve years in A.A. program. Since taking Mind Control, S has had one brief relapse of less than one hour's duration. No subsequent relapses.

Subject 13: No relapses since discharge from hospital rehabilitation program. Since Mind Control, S is progressively "getting it all together." Improvement is noted in areas such as work, family, etc.

Subject 14: Since taking the Mind Control course, S has had several relapses, from all of which he has recovered on his own. He has not been hospitalized for any of these relapses as was the case prior to taking Mind Control.

Subject 15: Eight years on and off A.A. program. Hospitalized four times prior to taking the Mind Control course. Intermittent slips or relapses during this interim. Since taking the Mind Control course, S has experienced four relapses, two of them requiring brief hospitalizations.

Mind Control was obviously a powerful boost in the struggles of all but the last of these 15 alcoholics.

This one small study, of course, is not enough to prove that Mind Control should now be accepted as an integral part of the alcoholic's treatment. However, the improved sense of well-being that has turned up so uniformly in before and after tests on students and psychiatric patients clearly suggests that those looking for better ways to help the alcoholic should give Mind Control a try.

There is another condition that involves shattered self-esteem, not as self-imposed as drug or alcohol addiction, but even more widespread—poverty. Causes of poverty and the remedies for it have been debated for as long as there have been human societies. Mind Control does not enter this debate, but it can be of immense help in persuading the poor to rally their strengths and help themselves.

This may sound to some as if the debate has already been entered—as if in persuading the poor to help themselves we are assuming that they are to blame for their own poverty. This is obviously untrue, but every poor person can help himself break out of his confines when he finds in Mind Control what all others find, greater ability to control his own life.

The first serious effort to find out how useful, if at all, Mind Control might be as part of a rehabilitation program in social work was a study of 41 men and women on welfare.

It is well known that a person who finds himself out of work suffers a blow to his self-esteem. This makes it more difficult for him to think and act his way out of his problem. A defeated, self-deprecating job applicant conducts lackluster interviews that prolong his unemployment, in turn lowering his self-esteem even more. This may ultimately lead to welfare. If something could intervene in this downward spiral and provide a realistic boost to self-esteem, the person would be in a more powerful position to help himself.

This, roughly, was the reasoning of Larry Hildore, director of the Ottawa County Department of Social Service in Michigan. He had taken the course himself and knew what the training could do. The only question in his mind was whether the results could be measured and what the measurements would look like.

To design the research project and do the testing, he and Dr. De Sau turned to Dr. James Motiff of the psychology department of Hope College in Holland,

Michigan. For the test, they chose the widely used six-page hundred-question Tennessee Self-Concept Test, which measures five aspects of a person's opinion of himself: physical self, moral/ethical self, personal self, family self, and social self. The test was given twice, once before the course and once after.

This alone might lead some to see the results as mere "Hawthorne Effect." In the mid-20's and early '30's, Western Electric Company launched a far-reaching research project to study various changes in working conditions that might improve employee morale at their Hawthorne Plant in Chicago. No matter what the company did, morale soared. They put something in; morale soared. They took it away; morale soared again. The conclusion was that folks are simply glad to be noticed, and this shows up in improved morale.

To measure this possible "Hawthorne Effect," Dr. Motiff tested another group of welfare recipients, who did not take the Mind Control course. They were tested twice, but unlike the Mind Control group, they experienced nothing special between the two tests. There was no "Hawthorne Effect."

Those who received Mind Control training wound up with radically different views of themselves—changes which in some cases exceeded chance by odds of millions to one. Changes were dramatic in all categories: The new graduates saw themselves as far better persons than they had earlier thought they were, and felt a new confidence in their ability to solve their own problems.

The degree of change led Dr. Motiff to exclaim that the data "are the most significant I have ever seen."

A report on the study said:

> There had been some concern as to how receptive a . . . [welfare] mother in the depths of her misery would [be] to a sudden input of Mind

Control, with its optimistic "better and better" philosophy. That concern was quickly washed away . . . on the second weekend. One hundred percent of those originally enrolled returned to finish the course, and the original shy silence had been replaced by a buzz of animated conversation that threatened to turn the session into a full scale revival meeting.

Almost everyone had something constructive to report . . . a new closeness to their children . . . a chronic headache gone . . . decreased frustration . . . lost weight. One radiant young mother used the Mirror of the Mind technique to find the answer to employment and saw only a hand writing a check. The next day she got the job she'd always wanted.

It is generally a state of mind, a damaged self-image, that puts a person in prison, and that coarsens and brutalizes him while he is there; and it is a state of mind that often ensures his quick return once he is "free." The kind of freedom that Mind Control could be expected to give a prisoner is the kind it can give the rest of us: the smashing of mental confines that are manifested to many of us "on the outside" as headaches, ulcers, insomnia, and failure in life's work, and to the prisoner as walls and bars as well.

Mind Control's limited experience in prisons indicates that it results in an environment that is less brutal. Time spent there is no longer empty hours snatched by law from a person's life, but a rich part of life itself—hours of growing and self-discovery. Mind Control may not make prison a happy hermitage, but it can make it a more civilized place in which to grow.

Although statistical studies have not been made, the personal experiences of the prisoners and their instructors are far more eloquent. Lee Lozowick, when he was

Mind Control's area coordinator in New Jersey (he resigned early in 1976 to establish Hohm, a spiritual community), taught the course seven times at Rahway State Prison—four times to a total of some sixty inmates, and three times to prison staff.

"There is no question," he said, "about the benefits the inmates and staff received from the course. You could see it in their faces." Officials were so impressed with Mind Control that prisoners who were studying for a college degree were given academic credit for the course.

Ronald Gorayeb, who succeeded to Mr. Lozowick's Mind Control post, offered the course to ten inmates at the Passaic County Jail in New Jersey. One man dropped the course when he was released from jail and wanted to return to complete it—prison officials had to say no. Another requested solitary confinement after the course to help him meditate—prison officials said yes. Still another, using the mental screen technique, programmed a job on the outside. He found one—all he needed for parole.

CHAPTER NINETEEN

MIND CONTROL IN
THE BUSINESS WORLD

Imagine believing in Murphy's Law—"If anything can go wrong, it will, and at the worst possible time"—then suddenly discovering that there is no such law but, instead, the cosmic Bill of Rights that José wrote about. You feel luckier because you are luckier.

Many Mind Control graduates say this is what happens in their working lives. The salesman finds his customers more open to him; the scientist finds sudden answers to perplexing problems; the professional athlete racks up better scores; the unemployed find jobs; the employed enjoy their jobs more.

"When I meet with Mind Control graduates throughout the company," said Michael Higgins, forty-four-year-old Director of Employment Development at the Hoffmann-La Roche, Inc., plant in Nutley, New Jersey, "I find a consistent positive attitude and cheerfulness reflected in these people, and I experience this on a continuing basis."

Hoffmann-La Roche is one of the world's giant pharmaceutical manufacturers. "This may surprise you, coming from a manufacturer of tranquilizers," Higgins said, "but we are open to alternative means of achieving better mental health, and this was one of our motivations for originally exploring Silva Mind Control in 1973."

Another thing that motivated Mr. Higgins to investigate the course is that few of the most effective employees of any company are fully as effective as they could be. What he found at Mind Control led him to plan a pilot project that would lead initially to a company-backed program, and from there build enough enthusiasm to take off on its own. He announced the plan, "signed up fifty people overnight," and turned to Reverend Albert Gorayeb, pastor of a church in neighboring Paterson, who is one of Mind Control's more charismatic lecturers.

The plan succeeded. Now, three years later, there are more than three hundred graduates at the plant—top executives, scientists, secretaries, engineers, laboratory assistants, and personnel managers. Some took the course under company sponsorship, many on their own.

"I was particularly fascinated by the research people who took the course. At first they were the most vigorous scoffers, but they turned out to be the most enthusiastic of all," Mr. Higgins said.

Here are some comments from Hoffmann-La Roche's Mind Control graduates, published in the plant's newspaper, *Inside Roche:*

From a merchandising director: "It gave me a new sense of awareness about myself and the importance of interacting and working with fellow employees. I am applying what I learned by trying to develop the ability to channel my interests and accomplishments so there is less wasted time and motion."

From an assistant biochemist: "My whole mental attitude has changed; as a result I'm convinced that good things really happen when you look at life positively.

It's amazing how much warmth flows between two people when you are pleasant and tolerant of each other."

From a personnel administrator: "It is one of the best things that has happened to me and I consider it a privilege to have been able to participate. The course, which emphasizes positive thinking, helped me develop an inner peace and build up my confidence."

From a plant services supervisor: "Mentally, I feel better—I don't worry as much or handle everything as an emergency, and I've learned to relax and control my headaches. The key to success is belief."

From a senior systems analyst: "Increased confidence and a general feeling of well-being are results of the course, which teaches us how to recognize parts of our nature that are usually ignored. For example, the program heightens sensitivity to other people and makes us more aware of intuitive experiences that the rational mind tends to deny."

A business built from the ground up with Mind Control techniques is the Idea Banque, Inc., in Chicago—a co-op for Mind Control graduates with marketable inventions. It started when Richard Herro, who is in charge of Mind Control activities in the Chicago area, posed a complex marketing problem to see if the kind of intuition sparked by Alpha and Theta could lead to practical answers. Mr. Herro, with ten years' experience as a marketing consultant behind him, already had a perfectly good answer—it had taken him ten years to work it out. Mind Control graduates came up with perfectly good answers too—in ten minutes.

"I pretty much expected something like this, but what I wasn't ready for was that the nontechnical people did far better on technical problems than experts. They aren't locked into logic and can explore more possibilities.

"I had to conclude," he said, "that the combined intelligence of twenty people at their level, tapping their creative imagination, is about a thousand times as effective as the intelligence of twenty people trying to reason their way to a solution."

Using the same problem-solving techniques himself, he invented and patented a new way of making prestressed concrete. Then Mind Control graduates began coming up with ideas of their own and needed marketing know-how. "That's how the Idea Banque was born," he explains.

Altogether, the Idea Banque, now in its second year, has eighteen inventions on or ready for the market and about a score in the works. One is a "leaf-eater," a lawn-mower attachment for making mulch of leaves. A firm which markets products by television bought two and a half million of them. Another is an adhesive patch for torn screens. Instead of being invisible, this one catches the eye. The "Bug Plug" is colored and shaped like a bug.

The company meets once a month for problem solving through meditation. Its members are those with ideas with a profit potential. They pay an initial fee plus a small monthly fee and share in the profits.

Another business group founded by Mind Control graduates in the Chicago area is, or was, an investment club. A stockbroker thought his new ability to move backward or forward in time could be put to advantage in selecting stocks. If in meditation you see a stock in the future, buy it now and sell it in the future. The plan appealed to Mr. Herro, and a club was formed. Mr. Herro, the broker, and other members were enthusiastic but not quite sure. Mind Control has solved a sweeping spectrum of problems but never, as far as anyone knew, the problem of accurately foreseeing the ups and downs of prices on Wall Street.

With this healthy skepticism, members held on to their cash during the first six months of weekly trial runs.

Each week the broker provided the names of ten stocks. The members, in Alpha, visualized themselves thirty days in the future. They saw themselves in a broker's office or reading a newspaper, learning how each of the stocks had done. When they returned to the present, in Beta, their findings were tallied. When the vote was 1½ to 1 in favor of a stock, a purchase was made—on paper.

At the very outset a problem cropped up. Members had to learn that cheery optimism, one of the marks of a Mind Control graduate, is often a poor guide to what the stock market will do. They started off seeing all the stocks rising. However, they learned quickly and were soon making "hits." The group's "portfolio" began to do better than the market average.

Another problem set in. With growing enthusiasm, the psychic investors began reading about the stocks they had selected, becoming more and more informed. They brought this objective information to their meditations and their paper profits dipped.

The answer to this was to give each stock a coded number so that no one would know which stock he was psychically studying. Results improved, once again ahead of market averages. Now, with six months of data proving that trained psychics can outpace the stock market, it was time to put up real money.

The transition from trial runs to real investing went smoothly. Members racked up real profits. When the market went down, so did their stocks, but not as much as the market as a whole. When the market rose, so did their stocks, even more than the market. However, after about a year, a hitch developed. The market went down more than up. The group's portfolio went down too, though not as sharply. Still, it was down, and the pride the group felt in outperforming the market was tempered by their losses.

Any sophisticated investor will tell you that money can be made instead of lost when the market is going down. Just sell short. You sell a stock now, even though you do not have it, then buy and deliver it later after the price goes down. Perfectly legal—but this is making a profit from others' losses or, to put it another way, having a vested interest in bad news—not for Mind Control graduates. The club was suspended.

As this is being written, the market is rising, and Mr. Herro reports the members may start again.

His interest in Mind Control's usefulness in business extends to sports, which, he says, is just as much a business as marketing new products and investing in the stock market. You may have heard that a number of the Chicago White Sox players took Mind Control. This was widely publicized in the summer of 1975, on CBS-TV's *60 Minutes* and NBC-TV's *Today* show. This was largely Mr. Herro's doing.

When the baseball season ended, he compared the players' individual scores—before Mind Control (1974) and after (1975). They all improved, most of them dramatically.

Among the most enthusiastic Mind Control graduates are salesmen. "I go into my level and visualize a successful call. The results have been remarkable. Every month I tell myself I'm going to produce X dollars, setting higher and higher goals, and I keep making them." This was said by a salesman for one of Wall Street's more prestigious firms. A vice-president of a small steel company said, "I tell myself, 'I'm going to sell this guy,' and it works. Now I'm recommending it [Mind Control] to my salesmen, my partners, even my children. I think everyone can benefit by it, and not solely in their work but in their personal lives as well."

In terms of numbers of reports from graduates, the most impressive results are in finding new jobs. The calm self-confidence that comes from Mind Control training probably accounts for this as much as any other factor—the self-assurance necessary to seek out a better job, the greater ease with which the graduate conducts job interviews, these alone can turn the tide in a person's career.

A photographer with a wife and two children suddenly lost his job, and he wrote to his lecturer:

> If this had happened five years ago, I would have hit the closest bar with all the justification in the world of getting roaring drunk . . . and crying in the beer of the unemployed guy beside me.
>
> NOW with Mind Control . . . separating clouds so I could shoot aerial photos without shadows on the ground, immediately healing dozens of cuts and bruises, and finding dozens of lost articles, just by looking on my screen, I wasn't the least bit worried about it being able to find me another job.
>
> All I did was enter my level and I saw myself going to college, which I thought was a riot in view of the fact that I am already a college graduate. . . . Investigation revealed, however, that I am actually eligible under the GI bill and will make $400 for the effort, and that plus $300 from unemployment will give me $700 take-home, which is $200 more than I was making when I had the

job. Plus the fact that I can now peddle to AP, UPI, and magazines.

Another person who recovered from a sudden job loss was a very new graduate in New York. He put in an angry phone call to José and said, "Now tell me about Mind Control!" José calmly told him to keep working with his mental screen and other techniques. Three days later he called José in a sharply different frame of mind. He'd just landed a job paying three times as much as the one he lost.

Perhaps the most colorful experience with Mind Control in business is reported by a man and his wife who open other people's safes. Here is how they do it: One of them goes psychically to the laboratory, evokes a vivid mental image of the safe and its owner, then turns back the clock and watches closely as the man opens his safe. The other, acting as orientologist, makes careful note of the numbers as they are called out. Later, in Beta, the psychic pays a house call and, in Beta, opens the safe for its amazed and grateful owner. The psychic, a licensed locksmith in the Midwest, is often called upon to open safes for owners who cannot recall their combination.

CHAPTER TWENTY

WHERE DO WE GO FROM HERE?

From the moment of your first accomplishment with Mind Control you will be launched on an odyssey of self-discovery. What you learn about yourself will be all good news. Finally, when you have made everything work for you as José has described in his chapters, several paths for future development will be open to you.

You may, through books or friends or other courses, try out still more techniques and add to the mental tools at your disposal. On the other hand, you may find that even a miracle repeated over and over becomes commonplace and, with the excitement of your new discoveries fading, you may slack off and drift back to where you were at the outset. Or, finding that one Mind Control technique works better for you than others, you may specialize in that one and make it a reliable part of your life.

None of these paths is the best for you.

If you begin a search for other techniques, you will find many that work. Chances are, the ones you find have already been researched by José and set aside in favor of those now in his course. Those who become technique collectors take time away from developing a few useful ones to the point of mastery. More on this later.

If you find that your excitement dims and you drift away from practicing Mind Control, you will not be alone. More important, your experience will not be a total loss. José has observed that, once acquired, Mind Control training is never completely lost and can be recalled and put to use in an emergency.

What many Mind Control graduates do is settle for one particular technique that works best for them. The more they use it, the better the results. However, there is a fourth way better than any of these three.

Mind Control is a very careful selection of mental exercises and techniques that reinforce each other. To ignore one because it does not work as well for you as another is to pass up the opportunity of truly full development. Dream Control reinforces your ability with the Mental Screen; the Mental Screen makes Dream Control more reliable and vivid. The course, and José's chapters here, are all of a piece; the whole is much greater than the parts.

Still, you may wonder where you go next when you have practiced it all and made it work.

Simply making Mind Control work is not enough. There are always degrees of control, subtleties of experience ahead of you.

A student once asked José, "At what point does a person know he has gotten out of Mind Control everything there is to get?"

"When you can convert all your problems into projects and make your projects work out the way you want them to," he answered. Then he paused a moment and added, "No . . . it goes deeper than that. When you realize what enormous powers we were all born with, when you see in your own experience that these powers can only be used constructively, you come to realize that there is a dignity and a purpose behind our presence on this planet. My own opinion is that the purpose we must serve is to evolve, and this evolution is now our own, individual responsibility. I think most people have a kind of weak hunch about this. The more you practice Mind Control, the stronger this hunch becomes until it becomes a firm certainty."

It is this depth of experience that awaits you—the "firm certainty" that there is a benign purpose behind everything. In Mind Control, this comes not as a mystical flash after years of life-renouncing meditation, but quite soon, out of the daily business of living more effectively—from the everyday details of life as well as its destiny-shaping events.

Let's take a very small incident, the kind a new Mind Control graduate might experience, and we will see how it becomes a step toward building this "firm certainty." The first thing a recent graduate did on returning home from vacation was to remove the film from his camera and then search his luggage for another roll of exposed film. He could not find it. The film was not a great loss, but an annoying one; it was a record of the first week of his vacation.

He went to his level and relived the moment he last put film in his camera; but all he saw on his Mental Screen was the camera itself on his coffee table, where he had put the first roll in, not the second. He stayed at his level and went from one picture-taking moment to another, but still no scene of his reloading the camera. Stubbornly, the coffee-table scene kept reappearing.

Convinced that his Mental Screen had failed, he turned in the one roll of film for developing. When it came back it contained all the photographs he had taken, from the beginning to the end of his vacation. There never was a second roll.

As small as this incident was, it provided the graduate with the first concrete reason he had encountered outside the class for having more confidence in his own mind. With a few more small incidents like this, then several major ones in which he helps not only himself but someone else as well, his view of himself and the world around him will change. His life will be changed because he will be on the brink of that firm certainty.

Along the way, he may achieve something like the following: A graduate who had been practicing Mind Control for several months had a daughter who was allergic to his family's two cats. Whenever she played with them she wheezed uncomfortably and broke out in a rash. He put the problem, then imagined the solution, on his Mental Screen during his meditations for about a week. The solution he imagined was his daughter playing with their cats, breathing easily, with no rash. One day he saw in real life what he had been imagining. His daughter was no longer allergic to cats.

Both these cases involved the Mental Screen alone. They were both successful, so, you might ask, why bother with other techniques?

In the first case, if the graduate had learned nothing except how to use his Mental Screen, it is just possible that he would have achieved the same results—assuming that he had simply triggered the recall of a "forgotten" fact and that Higher Intelligence did not come into play, which is far from certain.

However, the second case involved a broad range of Mind Control training—going to level, visualization exercises, Effective Sensory Projection for the telepathic transmission of healing, Dream Control, and case working, so that he could add a full measure of expectancy to his desire and belief.

With extensive practice, your mind will begin to take short-cuts. It will become sensitive to faint signals on important matters and will pass them on to you without your having to search for them. One Mind Control graduate's life may have been saved this way. She was meditating one morning just before going to work, using her Mental Screen to correct a small office problem, when a large black X blocked out the scene she was trying to create. Then it blocked out all other scenes connected with her office. A "hunch" too strong to ignore told her to avoid her office that day, and she happily stayed home. Later she learned that if she had gone to the office that day she would have walked into an armed robbery in which several persons were badly injured. This is the kind of information we would normally get with Dream Control, but the Mental Screen was what she was using and that is where it came through.

Here is another case, in which the mind was so trained that in a serious emergency it was brought under control by a graduate without taking time to go into Alpha. Many of the events described in the following letter were attested to by nine witnesses.

Wednesday, I came home from shopping, my arms loaded with bags. I opened the screen door, which swung back on me before I could open the inside door. Impatiently, I gave the door a hard push. To my horror, it slammed back fast, and the pointed door handle stuck in my arm below the elbow. I dropped the bags and slowly pulled the handle out of my arm. I could see down through layers and layers of tissue into a deep hole.

Then blood started to well up, filling the hole, flowing over. I didn't have time to feel faint. Instead, I concentrated intensely on stopping the bleeding. A great surge of joy shot through me when the bleeding stopped—I could barely believe my eyes!

While I was washing and cleansing the wound, the first pains came. I sat down and went to my level, trying to find out whether I should cancel a trip to Boston to hear Major Thompson at a Mind Control meeting and go to a doctor instead. But I felt a strong urge to go to Boston, also a strong urge to test my belief in having learned to control pain.

I worked on my pain incessantly on the way to Boston. But during the lecture it became so severe and my fingers so numb that even at my level I could hardly stand it. I felt guilty that I couldn't listen to the lecture—yet next day I was able to repeat it almost word for word.

While in such severe pain, I kept calling for help psychically over and over. Martha must have heard my cry because, after the lecture, as people wandered over to the coffee table, she insisted on seeing my "cut." When I raised the bandage, the wound was still gaping open. A piece of flesh had been somewhat dislodged when I pulled out the handle, and the skin around it was purplish black. She went for help and, having found out where the nearest hospital was, came back with Dennis Storin. I said I did not want to go to the hospital. I wanted Dennis to work on it, so we withdrew to a quiet corner where Dennis went to his level.

Once he started to work on the wound, my pain became so intense that I had to go to my level to work on it, too. As he began knitting the broken tissue together bit by bit, his fingers seemed to draw out the pain in huge waves. The wound became so sensitive I felt like screaming! I tried to concentrate on making the pain go away and on sending help to Dennis and to myself, over and over and over again—successfully combating the urge, undoubtedly conceived in Beta, to tell him to stop and let me go to an accident room. I really wanted it to work.

And, after hours, it seemed, I could feel the pain begin to subside. First, I felt about ten percent less pain, then about fifteen percent. When Dennis asked how it was, about a quarter of the pain had gone.

As we continued, the inner tissues mended. Then, as the outer layers began to mend, the pain became even more intense. Despite my concentration on the healing, I was slightly conscious of people moving around me—especially of someone standing behind me, taking away some of the pain when I needed it most desperately. I felt so grateful. Then the next waves started, and I had to concentrate hard on coping with them.

Then we worked on closing the deepest part of the wound. I felt people forming a circle around us to give us strength. I could feel the energy surging through me—it almost lifted me off the chair.

Dennis could feel it, too, and with the help of the others, the healing progressed much faster. Some of those in the circle later told me that they could see the wound closing, the swelling going down, the skin turning from an unhealthy purple to reddish-purple, to red, to pink, and, finally, the two outer layers of skin coming together like the well-cut pieces of a jigsaw puzzle.

When we got back to where my car was parked, my friends wanted to drive me to Warwick—they didn't want the wound to open up when I used my arm on the stick shift of the car. But I refused. I knew I would get home safely. And so I did—with absolutely no pain!

Next morning, I woke up in fine shape. My arm

felt as if I had been in a fight—I've never been beaten up, but I imagine it must feel like that! But there was no pain, and my arm looked great. I sat up in bed and saw our beautiful world bathed in brilliant sunshine. I felt as if I had been reborn!

As you can see, if you continue to explore the potentials of your mind, it will pay off in priceless ways. In this respect, says Dr. J. Wilfred Hahn, Mind Control's Director of Research, every Mind Control graduate becomes his own director of research.

"In what other field of research," he asked, "are expensive laboratories and sophisticated equipment so unnecessary? The most sophisticated research tool ever developed—one so remarkable that I am in awe whenever I think of it—is at your disposal and mine twenty-four hours a day: our minds. We are all, therefore, directors of research."

One important advantage that we have now is that, for the first time in the history of modern science, psychic research is becoming respectable. The danger of a serious investigator being put down as an irresponsible crackpot, as José was in his early days, is vastly reduced.

This danger, however, is not entirely behind us. There are physicians learning to use Mind Control in their practice, industrial scientists who use Dream Control to put them on the track of new products, men and women in all walks of life—some mentioned anonymously in this book—who say, "Don't use my name. My friends will think I'm crazy."

This is becoming more and more rare. Hundreds of thousands of Mind Control graduates proudly speak of what they are accomplishing with their training. Respected medical journals carry scientific and clinical papers on psychic healing and mind-body interactions.

Men and women in the public eye—members of the Chicago White Sox and performing artists such as Carol Lawrence and Marguerite Piazza (mentioned earlier), Larry Blyden, Celeste Holm, Loretta Swit, Alexis Smith, and Vicki Carr—all these have spoken out publicly of their Mind Control experiences.

Where do we go from here? Down a long path of exciting self-discovery. With each new finding you will be closer to the goal of the ultimate research project spelled out for us by William Blake:

> *To see a world in a grain of sand*
> *And a heaven in a wild flower,*
> *Hold infinity in the palm of your hand*
> *And eternity in an hour.*

APPENDIX I

THE MIND CONTROL COURSE AND THE ORGANIZATION BEHIND IT

José Silva

Now you know what Mind Control is all about and what hundreds of thousands of men and women are accomplishing with it. Because the movement is so widespread and fast-growing, it is obviously not possible to tell you everything that every graduate has gained from this training.

If you know any Mind Control graduates, you have probably heard a variety of reports on the benefits they are enjoying. Some use it for health, some to help them study, others in their business lives and family relationships, and many, who say little about it, use it to help others.

Given this variety of reports, you may wonder whether the course differs from one lecturer to another. No, it is the same throughout the world. As different as the lecturers may be—as different, for example, as you would expect a minister to be from a former stockbroker—and despite the vast freedom they are allowed in presenting the course, the mental training and exercises, and the results, remain identical.

What does differ is the personal needs of those who take the course. Not everyone has the same problems, the same needs. Each person, as time passes after he graduates, tends to focus on those parts of the training that confront most directly the problems he wants most to solve.

Later, as other problems arise, long-neglected parts of the course are put to work. The techniques, never forgotten, are easily recalled when they are needed. You will find this true when you have reread and put into practice the exercises in Chapters 3 through 14, and then later review them. Nevertheless, you may be tempted to say, "Well, my problem is such and such, so I'll just concentrate on that." The course, and the parts of it outlined in these chapters, fit together in meaningful ways that have been tested through research and long experience. One seemingly unrelated part reinforces all the others, including whichever one may interest you the most.

Some of what you would get if you took the course under a certified lecturer is omitted from my chapters here. Does this, you may wonder, change the course? It will change the course in two ways: The speed with which you will learn it all will be considerably slower—weeks with the book compared with forty-eight hours in a Mind Control classroom. Second, there is an energy transfer among people in a group which is a major part of the peak experience, or "high," you have read about. However, when you conscientiously learn all the exercises I have guided you through, you will be able to do everything a Mind Control graduate can do.

The reason some parts of the course are left out is not to deliberately withhold anything from you, but simply that they require a trained lecturer.

Many graduates find that the exercises and mental training become powerfully reinforced when they repeat the course long after taking it the first time. They are encouraged to do this (without cost), and as a result ten to twenty percent of a typical Mind Control class are repeaters. Many say the experience is even more intense the second time. If you go on to take the course, your first time will be a deeper experience because of your mastery of the techniques in this book.

Here, in outline, is everything Mind Control students go through in their classes:

Morning of the First Day

9:00 The day begins with a lecture to give students a general preview of the entire course.

10:20 Coffee break.

10:40 Questions, answers, and discussion, then a detailed preview of the first meditation.

11:30 The lecturer leads students for the first time to a meditative, or Alpha, level of mind. They may squirm or scratch as they wish, though at this and deeper levels the body requires less attention as it becomes more relaxed, particularly while experiencing the "ideal place of relaxation."

12:00 Coffee break.

12:20 Lecturer leads the students again into meditation, at a deeper level, though still within the Alpha range.

12:50 Questions and answers and a general sharing of experiences by the students.

1:00 Lunch break.

Afternoon of the First Day

2:00 Lecturer discusses the Building Blocks of Matter—atomic, molecular, and cellular—and the evolution of the human brain. The need for "mental housecleaning" is discussed in detail (see Chapter 8).

3:20 Coffee break.

3:40 The third meditation is explained in detail, along with a swifter method of reaching the Alpha level.

4:10 Students enter a still deeper level of mind and achieve still greater physical relaxation.

4:40 Coffee break.

5:00 The fourth meditation reinforces the previous three and previews the next one, when Dynamic Meditation begins with problem-solving techniques.

5:30 The students, many of them now relaxed more than they have ever been before, share their experiences and pose questions.

6:00 Dinner break.

Evening of the First Day

7:00 Three problem-solving techniques are described: how to get to sleep without drugs, how to awaken on time without an alarm clock, and how to overcome drowsiness and fatigue. Discussion follows.

8:20 Coffee break.

8:40 During the fifth meditation the lecturer helps students learn these techniques while they are at their Alpha and Theta levels.

9:10 The lecturer outlines the agenda for the second day, then describes Mind Control's techniques for programming dreams and controlling migraine and tension headaches. Questions and a discussion follow.

10:10 Coffee break.

10:30 The sixth meditation completes a day in which students have learned to meditate at deep levels of mind and to use these levels for relaxation and problem solving.

Morning of the Second Day

9:00 The lecturer briefly describes the day ahead and explains how to create and use the Mental Screen (Chapter 3). The lecturer then demonstrates his mastery of the Memory Pegs (Chapter 5).

10:20 Coffee break.

10:40 The Memory Exercise is explained and the next meditation is reviewed in detail.

11:00 The seventh meditation, during which—through Speed Learning (Chapter 6)—students begin to memorize the Memory Pegs and create their Mental Screen.

11:40   Coffee break.

12:00   During a brief lecture, students learn about the Three Fingers Technique and how to use it for improved memory (Chapter 5) and for Speed Learning (Chapter 6).

12:15   The eighth meditation conditions students to the Three Fingers Technique and teaches them to use it. The second morning ends with questions and answers and a general discussion of what has been accomplished.

1:00   Lunch break.

Afternoon of the Second Day

2:00   The second afternoon begins with an explanation of one of the key problem-solving techniques of Dynamic Meditation, the Mirror of the Mind—an elaboration of the Mental Screen. In addition, a deepening exercise, Hand Levitation, and a method for controlling pain, Glove Anesthesia, are discussed. A question period follows.

3:20   Coffee break.

3:40   Another question-and-answer period, followed by the ninth meditation, during which students learn the Mirror of the Mind. Discussion follows.

4:40   Coffee break.

5:00   The tenth meditation is the deepest yet. At these deeper levels the Memory Pegs are reinforced, and students practice the Hand Levitation and Glove Anesthesia exercises. The discussion period is largely a sharing of experiences.

6:00   Dinner break.

Evening of the Second Day

7:00   A lecture-discussion explores various beliefs and some research on reincarnation. The Glass of Water technique is explained as a method of triggering problem-solving dreams.

8:20 Coffee break.

8:40 After a brief question period, students learn the Glass of Water technique.

9:10 The lecturer explains how to use Mind Control to break unwanted habits (Chapter 9).

9:40 Coffee break.

10:00 The lecturer previews events of the third day and, after a brief question-and-answer period, begins the eleventh meditation for habit control. Finally, with a Mind Control graduate, he may demonstrate how cases will be worked on the fourth day. The students leave relaxed and with a growing sense of well-being.

Morning of the Third Day

9:00 This eventful day opens with a discussion of the many differences between Mind Control and hypnosis, particularly with respect to the spiritual dimension in which the students are about to function. Questions and answers.

10:20 Coffee break.

10:40 Students are told they are about to function psychically and as a first step will mentally project themselves from where they are to their own living room and then into the south wall of this room (Chapter 12).

10:55 In particularly deep meditation students vividly experience Effective Sensory Projection to their living room and into its south wall.

11:40 Coffee break, during which the students, with growing excitement, familiarize themselves with metal cubes (Chapter 12).

12:00 Lecturer explains that students will mentally project themselves into metal cubes to establish points of reference. In the thirteenth meditation, they experience the metals' color, temperature, odor, and sound when tapped.

This is followed by a spirited sharing of experiences.

1:00   Lunch break.

Afternoon of the Third Day

2:00   The lecturer discusses two new experiences in store for the students: projection into living plants, and deliberate shifting of time backward and forward. This is followed by a deeper exploration into the implications of Mind Control.

3:20   Coffee break.

3:40   The fourteenth meditation is explained. During this meditation students visualize a fruit tree in the various seasons, then mentally project themselves into its leaves. A sharing of experiences follows.

4:40   Coffee break.

5:00   The lecturer previews another major step forward: this one into a living animal.

5:15   During the fifteenth meditation students visualize a pet and mentally project themselves into it. Their sensations as they enter the pet's organs will soon be useful as reference points in working human cases. The discussion that follows is often the most animated so far.

6:00   Dinner break.

Evening of the Third Day

7:00   A lecture prepares students for objectively verifiable clairvoyant functioning, which they will do tomorrow. First requirement is a fully equipped laboratory (Chapter 12).

8:20   Coffee break.

8:40   Students are urged to exercise freedom and imagination in creating their laboratory and its instruments. During the sixteenth meditation the laboratory is mentally created. In most cases it remains basically unchanged years after the course, and becomes as familiar to the graduate as his own living room. An animated sharing of experiences and laboratory designs follows.

9:40   Coffee break.

10:00   Before the big day to come, the soon-to-be psychics will need their counselors for consultation in the laboratory. The lecturer explains how to evoke or create them, then answers students' questions.

10:15   The seventeenth meditation is a memorable one: Two counselors appear in the laboratory, where they will be available whenever the student needs them.

10:45   The day's final discussion is filled with exclamations as students share their colorful experiences. Many are surprised at who turned up as their counselors; others will have had genuine psychic experiences.

Morning of the Fourth Day

9:00   The day opens with a lecture on psychic and prayer healing, a preview of the events to come, and a general discussion.

10:20   Coffee break.

10:40   In deep meditation, the students, with the help of their counselors, examine portions of the body of a friend or relative to establish, for the first time, points of reference in the human body.

11:40   Coffee break.

12:00   During the nineteenth and final group meditation, students complete the psychic examination of their friend or relative.

1:00   Lunch break.

Afternoon and Evening of the Fourth Day

2:00   The lecturer gives students detailed instructions on how to work cases and, in pairs, they begin work—at first doubtfully, then with growing assurance, and finally with an exhilarating realization that they have been successfully trained to call on Higher Intelligence and function psychically whenever they wish.

As you read the above you were probably amazed at the frequency of the coffee breaks. Actually, very little coffee is consumed. These breaks have several important functions in the training. One is to allow students time to reflect on what they have experienced. Another is to give them plenty of unstructured time to become acquainted. This is part of the way a powerful group spirit develops—a collective psychic energy that grows as the course progresses, adding to everyone's confidence and success. It also allows students to stretch and to go to the bathroom. Finally, and not unimportant, it allows them to return to the Beta level, which adds to the depth of later meditations. For this reason, many lecturers call coffee breaks "Beta breaks."

The lecture material is developed largely by the lecturers themselves, around outlines provided by headquarters in Laredo. They draw heavily on their own backgrounds and experiences. However, all exercises and instructions the students hear while in meditation are delivered word for word as I prepared them myself.

After the students graduate, there is available to them a three-day graduate course taught by Dr. Wilfred Hahn (Director of Research), Harry McKnight (Associate Director), James Needham (Director of Graduate Training), and myself. This course sets forth the intellectual foundations of Mind Control training and provides some additional techniques.

Many Mind Control centers offer workshops of their own design. Some concentrate on working cases, others on memory improvement, subjective communication, healing, and sparking creativity.

Some graduates form organizations of their own—cottage groups—and meet regularly in members' homes for explorations in meditative technique.

The Mind Control organization is a fairly simple one. The Institute of Psychorientology, Inc., is the parent organization. The course is taught by Silva Mind Control International, Inc., in 34 nations. One of its divisions, Silva Sensor Systems, makes tapes, study aids, and research equipment available to students and graduates, and manages the Mind Control Bookstore. The Institute of Psychorientology, Inc., publishes a newsletter for graduates and holds conventions, graduate courses, seminars, and workshops. Mind Control research is conducted by Psychorientology Studies International, Inc., a nonprofit organization. SMCI Programs, Inc. concentrates on marketing relaxation seminars, some of which use biofeedback custom tailored for executives.

APPENDIX II

SILVA MIND CONTROL AND THE PSYCHIATRIC PATIENT

*Clancy D. McKenzie, M.D., and
Lance S. Wright, M.D.*

In November 1970 we attended a Silva Mind Control class in Philadelphia because we were curious about some of their claims. As the course progressed, it became apparent to us there were three persons who were definitely emotionally disturbed and a fourth whose stability was in question. What was the reason? Did the course precipitate emotional illness? Had they been ill when they arrived? Were disturbed persons attracted to the course?

We discussed the possibilities with our colleagues, and many of them speculated that the course could precipitate acute psychosis in unstable individuals. This sounded plausible. It is generally accepted that anything that facilitates regression may bring about an acute psychosis in someone who is so inclined. Sensory deprivation and hallucinogenic drugs can bring on psychotic-like behavior, and even such techniques as biofeedback and hypnosis can alter the psyche as well. Most psychoanalysts do not recommend

* Clancy D. McKenzie, M.D.—Director of Philadelphia Psychiatric Consultation Service. Attending Psychiatrist, Philadelphia Psychiatric Center.

Lance S. Wright, M.D.—Senior Attending Psychiatrist, Institute of Pennsylvania Hospital. Associate Professor of Child Psychiatry, Hahnemann Medical College.

formal psychoanalysis on the couch for the psychotic patient because it produces further regression. It remains undetermined how great this risk factor is, but there are claims that all these procedures have ended up in psychosis.

In 1972 two thousand students at a Philadelphia high school went through the SMC training with no psychiatric casualties, according to a responsible school official. This aroused our curiosity in another way. Since adolescents are already in a state of ego instability, hearsay claims that the course was dangerous for unstable individuals were thrown into doubt. Our dilemma was compounded. We saw three disturbed individuals in a group of 30 and did not know if they had been made better or worse. There were claims by some members of the scientific community of large numbers becoming psychotic. The high-school study indicated this was not the case. In fact, some of our own patients, even severely disturbed ones, had taken the course and appeared to be dramatically benefited by it. A review of the literature showed opinions but no actual studies.

Clearly, the only way to proceed was to evaluate and test individuals before and after the training. Over the next four years 189 of our psychiatric patients voluntarily went through the Silva Mind Control training while they were in therapy. Particular emphasis was given to a group of 75 patients who were diagnosed as psychotic, borderline, or psychosis in remission, before entering the course. These we called the severely disturbed group. At some time in their lives, 60 of them had either been psychotic or had been hospitalized.

The 75 included everyone from the severely disturbed group found in McKenzie's practice over the last four years who agreed to attend the SMC course (66 patients) and a sampling found in Wright's practice over the last four years (9 patients). There were 7 severely disturbed patients who refused to attend, even when the course was offered free. They were not more disturbed than the ones who did attend. Those who attended included the most disturbed; those who refused simply tended to be more rigid and inflexible in their thinking. Presumably they would not represent persons who might get into difficulty during the course, because they were not likely to take the course in the first place.

Initially patients from the severely disturbed group were sent to the course one at a time and with great caution. During the initial part of the study the patients were sent during a time of their remission. As the study progressed, however, the patients were sent during less-stable periods of their illnesses. Toward the end of the four-year period, 17 were sent while they were actively psychotic and delusional, and sometimes 10 or more went through the course at once.

In addition to their ongoing psychiatric treatment and evaluation, 58 of the 75 were given the Experiential World Inventory questionnaire before and after the course. The EWI is a 400-item questionnaire designed to measure reality perception. Drs. El-Meligi and Osmond, authors of the questionnaire, attempted to put the Rorschach in question-and-answer form, and arrived at a sensitive test for the marginal individual.

The primary purpose of the study was to find out which patients might become more disturbed with the training. In that regard the results were startling because only one patient became appreciably more disturbed after the course. He was a twenty-nine-year-old catatonic schizophrenic patient who became upset two weeks after the course when he stopped taking his medication and began dating for the first time in his life. He was also the only patient who scored appreciably worse on the EWI after the course. He did not require hospitalization.

Two other patients, one who had experienced psychotic depression and one with involutional depression, showed an increase in depression following the course, perhaps in contrast to the way they had felt during the training. The high feeling during the course was a marked contrast to their depressive state, and the experience was like taking a headache away from a person who had had it all his life.

If it returned it was more noticeable. However, these patients did score better on the EWI afterward, and they were able to make use of the training. The involutional depressed patient was able to use the Mind Control programming later the same week and function with less anxiety at work; and the person with a history of psychotic depression was able to work through things in therapy she had previously been unable to handle.

Twenty-six other depressed patients, including involutional, psychotic, schizo-affective, and manic-depressive types, were much less depressed after the course and showed no harmful effects.

One woman reported a sudden feeling of sadness during one of the relaxations. A man, not included in the 75, dropped out after the second day because he had flashbacks of unpleasant Vietnam experiences. His condition was not thought to be worse than when he began, but he did not return for further evaluation. (The relaxation puts persons in touch with feelings. Usually, because the mood of the group is high and the focus is positive, the feelings are of warmth and love, but on infrequent occasion persons evoke sadness and unhappy memories.)

Still another patient (not in the severely disturbed group) was afraid of the things to be done on the last day of the course, and after a bad dream did not go to the last day.

A paranoid schizophrenic man, age thirty, demonstrated great exuberance, approaching cyclothymic proportions, after the course. He tried various Mind Control techniques to determine what to do with the rest of his life, and spent many hours checking out possibilities from programmed dreams. This was seen as an increase of compulsive defenses. Nevertheless, as a result of his heightened activity, he was able to go back to school to earn his Ph.D. He also was able to discuss a delusional system he had experienced several years before, when he thought he was sent telepathically on a mission to kill someone. If he had not taken the course, this might never have been brought up and resolved.

In comparison with the relatively few and minor negative

effects of the course, the positive effects and results would require a book to describe. The most consistent finding was one we were not looking for and did not expect. In almost every instance there was an increase in reality perception. Of the 58 who took the EWI, one became appreciably worse, 21 remained about the same, and 36 demonstrated an impressive increase in reality perception. Of the 21 who remained about the same, 15 had scores that moved in the healthy direction.

The average scores of the first 20 women who took the course were sent to Dr. El-Meligi, co-author of the EWI questionnaire. He lauded the dramatic changes that took place after the Silva Mind Control training and said that in some categories the before and after scores were like those of a person during and after a bad LSD trip (see charts A and B). In each of the eleven categories there was consistent improvement. Individual scores were more impressive (charts E, F, and G). Composite scores of the 50 percent of the men and women who improved the most are indicated in charts C and D. It is thought that no conventional psychotherapy could produce as much change in a week; indeed, it might have required months or years of therapy.

One involutional paranoid woman's scores changed as much with the one-week course as they had on another occasion with eleven electroshock treatments and twelve weeks of hospitalization. After the one-week course, she was able to get on a bus by herself for the first time in four years.

Another woman, who was paranoid schizophrenic and acutely delusional, maintained some of her delusional thoughts after the course, but was able to go repeatedly to her "Mind Control level" to examine these thoughts, and each time arrive at clear, rational ideation.

Another woman, with an acute undifferentiated schizophrenic reaction, was too disturbed to fill out the EWI. She was given her choice: shock treatment or Mind Control. At the end of the course there was clinical improvement, and she not only could fill out the EWI but she scored quite well on it.

Still another, a hypochondriacal woman with a history of twenty operations, was about to have another. While the internal-medicine specialists were still checking out the heart and kidneys, she used a Mind Control technique to program a dream that diagnosed an intestinal obstruction at the ileocecal junction. She discovered from the same dream that she had produced the obstruction and how and why. Mind Control techniques enabled her to release the obstruction in a sudden, unexplained way one hour after the diagnosis was confirmed at the surgical hospital. The exact location of this obstruction was confirmed from records of previous surgery.

Another very distracted twenty-one-year-old woman was dangerously suicidal and in the early phases of an acute psychosis. The patient had assured us there was nothing we could possibly do that would help, and that she probably was just going to kill herself. We sent her to the Mind Control course under careful monitoring. Much to our surprise, she became remarkably calm, was more rational, her thought processes no longer raced in all directions at once, and she was less pessimistic. Hospitalization and high doses of medication could not have calmed her as much. She repeated the course two weeks later and again improved. She had changed dramatically for the better.

Yet another very delusional individual, who thought he could shrink people, took the course while hospitalized, returning each day to the hospital. Although he continued to think he could shrink people, he was remarkably calmed, the affect was improved, other parts of the delusional system were fading, and he no longer spent hours ruminating over the meaning of simple parables. He took the course during his sixth week of hospitalization, and the changes were more dramatic than during all of the previous five weeks. (See chart E).

An involutional paranoid woman was back to her normal self after the course. Several others had a better understanding of their illnesses as a result of portions of the course.

Clinically, the severely disturbed group as a whole showed an impressive change. Only one became more upset. All the others benefited to some degree from the training. There was an increase in emotional energy after the course and an improvement in affect. Many persons with flat affect showed enthusiasm for the first time. They had a more positive outlook about their future, and for some there was a better understanding of their psychotic processes. Even some who maintained delusional thought were able to evaluate their ideation at the "Mind Control level" and arrive at clarity and understanding.

There was a greater relaxation and lessening of anxiety. Patients learned to rely on their own inner resources to understand, cope with, and solve problems, and being able to do so gave them more self-confidence.

Some of the patients who had been psychotic found that their illness had enhanced their ability to function in an altered state of consciousness, and this added meaning to their prolonged illness and meaning to their lives.

Neurotic patients (114 of them) showed no negative effects clinically. Six of them took the EWI. Their scores improved, but not as much as the severely disturbed group's, because their first scores were already so near the healthy end of the scale. Invariably the neurotic patients seemed to benefit from SMC training. Those who continued to practice the techniques after training were able to alter their lives greatly, and even those who did not practice the techniques steadily were able to use them in times of personal crisis: when they had to cope with stress or had important decisions to make. For all it seemed to be a mind-expanding experience, a revelation that they could use their minds in new ways. Group enthusiasm mounted toward the end of the course, and most persons experienced a higher and more positive emotional level.

In general, both the neurotic and psychotic groups improved after the course, as demonstrated on psychological examination and as determined clinically. Only one out of 189 patients became appreciably worse.

II

Data from any research have to be evaluated in light of all conditions present, the tests and criteria used, and the care that goes into the study. Therefore, we will try to point out all the factors we are aware of that might have influenced the result.

From the standpoint of research, we wanted to know what effect the training had on disturbed individuals. As physicians, we wanted our patients all to get well. This undoubtedly had some bearing on the result, as they surely sensed this. We believe our optimism carried over in some way; this is an integral part of our everyday therapeutic effort.

Initially with some of the psychotic patients we waited until they were well stabilized before sending them through the course, but eventually patients were sent in acutely psychotic states.

The EWI test was thought to be a sensitive indicator of reality perception, and we found that the scores matched the clinical findings. Dr. El-Meligi confirmed that our clinical observations were consistent with the changes reflected by the EWI scales. The only patient who became appreciably more disturbed was the only one whose score became appreciably worse. The ones whose scores dramatically improved consistently showed remarkable clinical improvement as well.

The authors of the EWI believe that the test is repeatable and can be given over and over again. We did not initially test to see whether any of the changes noted were related to some repeatability factor. We tried to give the test the week before and the week after the training, but this was not always accomplished. More recently, in seven cases the test was given twice the week before and once the week after, to determine whether there is any repeatability factor. The ratio of "wrong" answers on the three tests was 100:92:65. Thus the difference between the first two tests was nominal compared with the change after the SMC training.

Counterbalancing any repeatability factor is the fact that there were many answers expected after but not necessarily before the training that would earn negative points. For example, two of the questions were "Can you read persons' minds?" and "Have you had a religious experience recently?" An affirmative answer to either earns a negative point. The course teaches persons to function psychically, and most persons become convinced they experience ESP; and for some the experience is almost a religious one. Thus we would have expected a worse performance after the course instead of a better one.

Summarizing the reliability of the EWI, a repeatability factor was nominal and was counterbalanced by another factor that caused a worsening of the score. The test was thought to be sensitive and reliable, and results corresponded with clinical evaluation as well as with how the patients felt subjectively.

For the purpose of the study we decided that anyone who became disturbed within a three-week period following the course would be considered a casualty, whether or not there were other factors contributing to the illness.

With any group of 75 highly disturbed patients followed over a period of three weeks, we might expect one or more to become more disturbed. This might happen even if they are in treatment and not exposed to a regressive experience. The fact that all patients were in treatment at the time of this study, and at times were given direction and reassurance, undoubtedly was supportive and perhaps prevented illnesses from occurring. But we believe that this supportive therapy could not of itself account for the dramatic positive changes that took place.

III

It is our experience that acute psychotic illness has an early origin, with a pathological mother-infant relationship in the first two years of life, often reinforced by subsequent trauma. This predisposition requires a precipitating factor in the person's current life situation to cause him to regress and re-experience the feelings and reality of the distant past. Usually the precipitating factor is a severe rejection or separation from an important person. The cause is early. The precipitating factor is current. Beyond this there may be a facilitating mechanism, such as hallucinogenic drugs, contact with original family, and other processes that foster regression. Thus we differentiate among (1) origin or predisposition, (2) precipitating factor, and (3) facilitating mechanisms. Psychosis can be likened to most natural processes that have an origin, a triggering mechanism, and facilitating mechanisms.

All psychotics we have treated became ill as a result of a rejection, separation, threatened loss (real or imagined), diminished attention, etc., triggering an unconscious fear of abandonment. In several hundred psychotic patients over the last ten years, the authors cannot recall any that did not experience some relative degree of loss or separation, even if this was only implied. The twenty-nine-year-old catatonic who became worse during the study, for example, was in conflict with his mother, who he thought would disapprove of his dating. This served as a precipitating cause, triggering regression to age one, when he perceived disapproval as impending abandonment and death.

If the Silva Mind Control course were to produce psychosis in an individual, it would be acting as a facilitating mechanism, which would have to be combined with a precipitating cause in a vulnerable person. We cannot recall seeing any patient whose psychotic process was produced by a facilitating mechanism alone. Although we do not doubt that this is possible, it must be relatively rare.

IV

What is Silva Mind Control?
Silva Mind Control is a forty-hour course consisting of thirty hours of lecture and ten hours of mental exercises.

The mental exercises not only teach persons how to relax the mind and body, as do other approaches such as bio-feedback and Transcendental Meditation, but they go one step beyond. They teach persons how to function mentally when they are at the relaxed level.

The entire course consists of techniques for using the mind in beneficial ways. After experiencing this ourselves and witnessing many others using it, we have no doubt about the superior ability of the mind to function when the person is using specific techniques in an alert relaxed state. It is similar to the state Sigmund Freud described in his paper on listening; like the state Brahms went into for creating his compositions, or the state Thomas Edison described for arriving at new ideas.

The course teaches a quick, easy method for going to this level of relaxation at any time. Trainees practice visualizing, imagining, and thinking at this level of consciousness, until they learn to function there mentally. They capture a wider range of brain activity for conscious use. They have an expanded range of consciousness. Instead of just day-dreaming when they are relaxed, they can use their minds effectively at that level. Instead of being in a light slumber, they can have awareness and use of the mind at that level too. Instead of just dreaming at night, they can use the dream state to solve problems and arrive at answers the mind is not capable of at any other time.

When persons learn to function mentally at the deeper levels of relaxation of mind and body, creativity is enhanced. Memory is improved, and persons are better able to solve problems. From the altered state, they are able to direct the mind to do what they desire, and thus control of such habits as smoking is made easier.

Continued practice at the relaxed level has an effect on the thought processes of everyday life as well—i.e., persons have access to their "level" without being there, like a musician who no longer has to concentrate on the music to know when a wrong note is played.

The mind has great capabilities, but at its normal level of functioning it is constantly bombarded by various stimuli at once: thoughts, wishes, needs, desires, noises, lights, pressures, conflicts, stresses of all sorts; it is not free to direct more than ten percent of its attention to any one thing. At the relaxed level it is. But persons ordinarily are at that level only when they are falling asleep, and they have not practiced using that level. Most often they do not even know that it exists and can be used.

Once a person experiences the results obtained from this level of consciousness, he never attempts to make important decisions or solve problems without using it.

The course most importantly teaches a person to use this level of mind. In addition to teaching persons to think while in the state of relaxation, the course teaches special techniques for habit control, problem solving, goal achievement, memorizing, health care, pain control, sleep and dream control, etc.

Mind Control is not hypnosis; it more nearly approaches self-hypnosis. Persons learn to get a fuller attention of the mind, perhaps because it is no longer bombarded by as many external stimuli when it is relaxed. With this fuller attention, they are better able to direct the mind to do what they want it to.

Another large portion of the course is learning to repeat beneficial phrases to oneself while at this level of mind-body relaxation. This is thought to have a powerful effect. Positive thinking is always valuable, but positive thinking in the relaxed state is immeasurably more so.

The last portion of the course deals with parapsychology; almost all persons report having ESP experiences during the course. This is so common that Mind Control guarantees a full refund if trainees do not feel they have experienced clairvoyance on the last day.

V

Why does Mind Control help the mental patient?

Early in the study we stopped speculating on why Mind Control might harm the mental patient and turned our attention to why it helped.

We do not know all the answers, but we think we are in a better position to speculate than those who have not carefully evaluated patients before and after the training.

The mobilization of energy may be an important factor. Freud said, in "Analysis Terminable and Interminable," that the effectiveness of a therapy of the future may depend primarily on the mobilization of energy. Persons are highly energized by the end of the course.

The positive attitude and optimism generated in the course must have a beneficial effect on the patient. Perhaps telling oneself beneficial phrases while at the relaxed level does effectively program the mind in a way that goes beyond simple positive thinking.

Relaxation diminishes anxiety and therefore decreases symptomatology. A person cannot be in a relaxed state of mind and body and be extremely anxious or conflicted at the same time. Functioning at that level is thought to produce the same carry-over effect of relaxation throughout the day as noted in TM.

The mood of the Mind Control group is high, and persons experience greater feelings of warmth and love while at the relaxed level. Perhaps the love energy plays an important part. Persons in love are generally not troubled by things that might otherwise bother them.

Since persons at the relaxed level are not in as much conflict, the early defenses of emotional distancing are not as necessary. Therefore affect is improved. They are more in touch with their feelings and more in touch with reality.

They have captured a wider range of brain activity for reality testing. Perception is improved at the relaxed level of mind and body, and clear thought and judgment are enhanced.

Special techniques help patients to solve some of their own problems, and they are able to program for relaxation and better feeling to last throughout the day. To be able to rely more on their own inner resources gives them more confidence. The therapists trust the answers they get at the altered state, and this adds to the patients' confidence.

A group phenomenon is present. The good emotional

feeling of the group is contagious and carries over even to the most disturbed.

The parapsychological part of the course helped some of the disturbed patients in an unexpected way. Many who were pushed to the outer reaches of the mind reported frequent paranormal experiences that psychotherapy did not explain. It was only in the parapsychological part of the course that they gained understanding. One of the stated purposes of deep psychotherapy is to make conscious what was unconscious. Expanding the range of consciousness and exploring the parapsychological aspects of the mind served this very same purpose. Patients felt relieved to uncover this aspect of their mental processes and found it to be real and accepted.

Because emotional illness helped them experience paranormal phenomena, this added meaning to their prolonged illnesses and meaning to their lives.

The therapist learned to apply Mind Control techniques to psychotherapy, helping the patients further.

VI

Summary and Conclusions:

Seventy-five highly disturbed patients were sent through Silva Mind Control training to determine which patients might get into difficulty. Only one became appreciably more disturbed. The most consistent finding was a dramatic increase in reality perception, as determined clinically and on objective psychological testing.

It is important to note that all the disturbed patients from one psychiatric practice were asked to go through the course, which meant that this was a complete sampling from one psychiatric-patient population. No one was withheld. Therefore the results do not apply to selected individuals only.

Silva Mind Control is not a psychotherapy. It can be used as a tool in any psychotherapy, particularly if the therapist is familiar with the course and not antagonistic toward its concepts. It provides the patient with an enhanced ability to use the mind and apply himself to whatever therapy he is in.

Psychotics have been helped so dramatically (at least when the patient is in treatment and the psychiatrist understands the course) that Dr. McKenzie now insists all his psychotic patients attend, while under his care and supervision.

Because of the dramatic improvement in most of the disturbed individuals, and because the training can be applied to large groups at once, the authors foresee an application as an ancillary form of treatment in the hospital setting.

The course was found to be safe and potentially beneficial for neurotics. It was relatively safe and definitely beneficial for the highly disturbed individual, when under the care of a psychiatrist familiar with the program. Both clinical and objective psychological data show that the benefits far outweigh any negative effect.

CHART A:

Average difference in T scores before and after SMC t~~~~
ing, for 38 women from the highly disturbed group.

There are improvements in all eleven scales, including ~~~~
euphoria scale. A lower score indicates improvement, e~~
cept on the euphoria scale, where a higher score indicat~~
that the patient feels better and is more optimistic.

The scales are as follows: *1. Sensory perception* consist~~
of items which describe the external world through direc~
sense experience, utilizing all sensory modalities. *2. Time*
perception samples phenomena related to subjective time
in four categories: change in experience of time flow:
temporal discontinuity; orientation, including mode of
engagement in past, present, and future; experiential age or
awareness of one's age and identification with or alienation
from one's generation. *3. Body perception* covers three
aspects of experiencing one's body: emotive aspects, hypochondriacal complaints, perceptual aspect. *4. Self-percep-*
tion includes emotive tendencies toward self-expression of
one's self-esteem and identity problems. *5. Perception of*
others is represented by five different patterns: dehumaniza-
tion of people, ascribing unusual powers to people, feelings
of change, ideas of reference, anthropomorphic tendencies
in relating to animals. *6. Ideation* focuses on pathology as
reflected in one's experience of his own thinking process
or its content, and it deals with various categories such
as: deficit in thinking process, disorganization, change
in thinking habits or ideology, intellectual omnipotence,
change in rate of thinking, and presence of bizarre ideas.
7. Dysphoria taps three levels of dysphoric affect; somatic,
emotional, and intellectual. In addition, it contains items
concerned with death wishes and self-destructive tendencies. *8. Impulse regulation* contains items emphasizing def-
icits of volition or will as an experience rather than actual
loss of control. The three classes of phenomena represented are: manifestations of hypertonicity; work inhibi-
tions and problems of decision making, compulsivity, and

complete suspension of action; asocial, antisocial, or bizarre impulses.

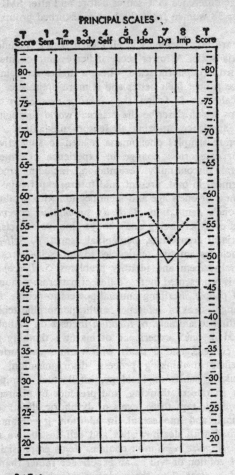

PRINCIPAL SCALES

	1	2	3	4	5	6	7	8	
Score	Sens	Time	Body	Self	Oth	Idea	Dys	Imp	Score

1st Test

2nd Test

3rd Test

ADDITIONAL SCALES

CHART B:

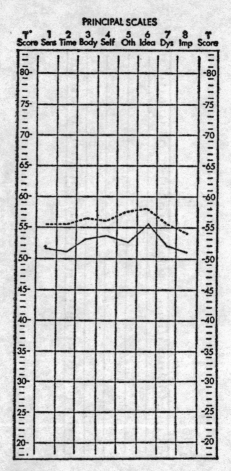

PRINCIPAL SCALES

1st Test
2nd Test
3rd Test

Average difference in T scores before and after SMC training, for 20 men from the highly disturbed group.

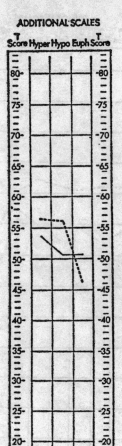

CHART C:

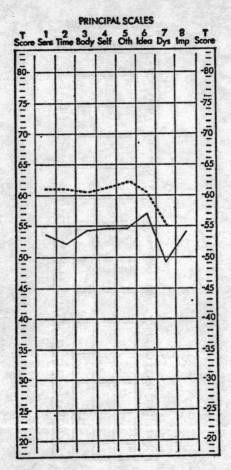

PRINCIPAL SCALES

Average difference in T scores for 19 of the 38 women in the highly disturbed group whose scores changed the most.

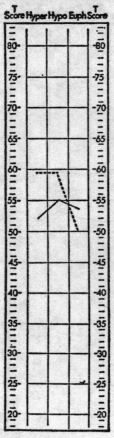

CHART D:

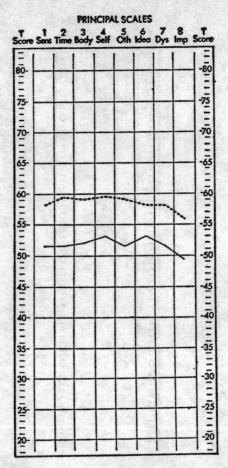

PRINCIPAL SCALES

1st Test ___ __ __ __ __ __ __ __ __
2nd Test ___ __ __ __ __ __ __ __ __
3rd Test ___ __ __ __ __ __ __ __ __

Average difference in T scores for the 10 of the 20 men in the highly disturbed group whose scores changed the most.

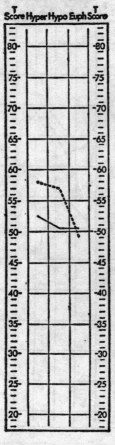

CHART E:

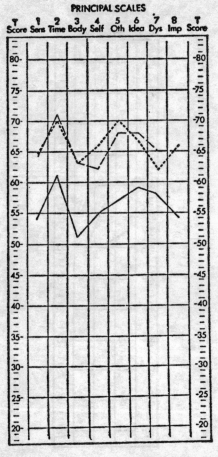

PRINCIPAL SCALES

An acutely psychotic patient tested twice the week before and once the week after Mind Control. Note the similarity of the two scores prior to SMC training, as compared with the score after.

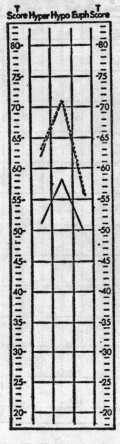

CHART F:

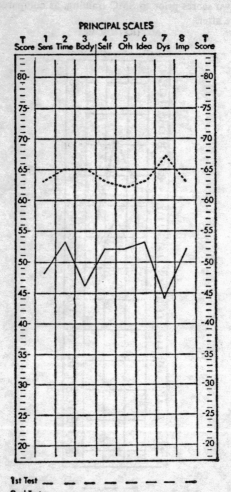

PRINCIPAL SCALES

| T Score | 1 Sens | 2 Time | 3 Body | 4 Self | 5 Oth | 6 Idea | 7 Dys | 8 Imp | T Score |

1st Test — — — — — — — — — —
2nd Test — — — — — — — — — —
3rd Test — — — — — — — — — —

One more of the highly disturbed group tested the week before and the week after SMC training.

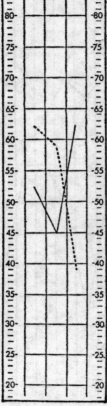

ADDITIONAL SCALES

CHART G:

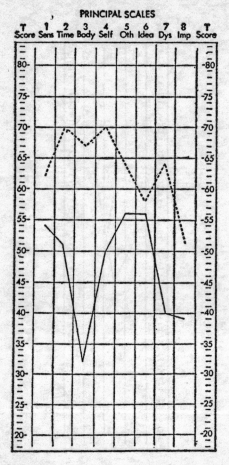

One more of the highly disturbed group tested the week before and the week after SMC training.

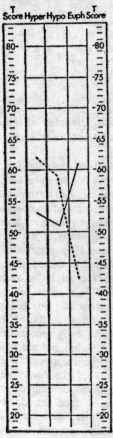

INTRODUCTION

J. W. Hahn, Ph.D., Director of Research
Silva Mind Control International

Until recently, scientists have been extremely critical of reports claiming that Yogis have learned to deliberately regulate their heartbeat, body temperature, and other internal body processes normally considered to be of an involuntary nature. Largely ignored also were reports that some subjects in deep states of hypnosis (an altered state of consciousness) could by suggestion be made to effect changes of a physiological nature normally considered not to be under voluntary control: for example, the raising of blisters and control of heart rate.

With the introduction of (bio)feedback techniques, the scientist has come to recognize during the last several years that almost any internal body process can be brought under control. Biofeedback techniques are based on the principle that we learn to respond correctly if we are immediately informed (feedback) of the correctness of the response or how close we are to responding correctly.

Using rewards as a feedback device in animals, psychologist Dr. Neal Miller, currently of Rockefeller University, demonstrated that heart-rate changes could be achieved by voluntary control. Dr. Elmer Green, at the Menninger Foundation, showed that by using biofeedback, humans could learn to differentially control the temperature of their hands—either hand hot, the other cold.

In the wake of brain-wave biofeedback experiments of Dr. Kamiya, of the Langley Porter Neuropsychiatric Institute, researchers have shown that these methods are effective in teaching individuals to control their brain-wave Alpha rhythm (8–13 Hz) voluntarily.

Other less laboratory-oriented techniques have also been used to control internal body organs. For instance, the technique of transcendental meditation attempts to produce a relaxation of internal organs including the brain.

Another system by which subjects can produce relaxation and control of brain waves is Silva Mind Control. Persons who have taken the Silva Mind Control courses report a sensation of deep relaxation and a belief that they can control their brain waves. These claims were tested in 1971 by Dr. F. J. Bremner, psychologist at Trinity University in San Antonio, Texas. It appeared that people trained in this way can indeed control their brain waves and produce Alpha rhythm when they choose to do so. This was determined in a study in which a group of twenty untrained students volunteered for an experiment in brain-wave control. Half of the students were conditioned by a method similar to Pavlov's method of conditioning dogs. That is, when the subjects heard a click it signaled that a strobe light would elicit an Alpha frequency response in the EEG. Soon the click also elicited the Alpha frequency pattern in the subjects' EEG readout.

The other ten subjects were trained by Mr. Silva with the Mind Control method. Both groups showed EEG changes in the direction predicted: that is, both groups increased the percentage of Alpha frequency in their EEG's.

At a later time a second experiment was done using subjects with considerable practice in the Silva method. These subjects could start and stop Alpha frequency responses at will and could carry on a conversation while generating Alpha rhythm. One further test was made on these more practiced subjects. Since these subjects had also had considerable experience in ESP exercises (case working), EEG's were recorded while they engaged in ESP exercises.

These EEG patterns also showed a high incidence of Alpha frequency.

It seems from these studies that with training, man can exercise a good deal of voluntary control over his internal organs. This holds true for the brain if we accept the electrical responses of that organ as being an indicator of its function. It also suggests that much more research is needed to determine the correlates of the physiological and mental-emotional states and the training procedures required to make the most of voluntary psycho-physiological self-regulation.

A better understanding of the significance of Silva Mind Control training may be emerging from research on the physiology of the brain, as reported by neurobiologist Dr. Rodger W. Sperry and his colleagues in Los Angeles. These and other scientists have developed laboratory and clinical evidence for the existence of two distinct kinds of consciousness functioning separately but simultaneously within the brains of humans. The one kind of consciousness deals with sequential, logic-dependent thinking activities such as mathematics and speech. It is functionally a product of the left hemisphere of the cortex. The other kind is associated with the right hemisphere and accounts for holistic and spontaneously creative, intuitive thinking, with an appreciation for spatiality and music.

The left-hemisphere consciousness dominates most of our everyday living and is favored even by the educational system as well as by the societal attitudes of the Western world. It is objectively oriented, and usually associated with the generation of much Beta brain-wave activity. Right-hemisphere consciousness seems to be primarily subjective, receives secondary consideration in our education, and finds its greatest expression in the arts. It is generally accompanied by Alpha or Theta brain-wave emanation.

Silva Mind Control trains individuals to maintain speech and other Beta thinking activities at Alpha as well as indulge in Alpha thinking processes of a creative, intuitive nature as part of a *deliberate* undertaking to provide for more equal distribution of function between left and right hemispheres. It helps balance an otherwise unequal preoccupation with left-hemisphere function when undertaking to solve problems. It would seem to accomplish a more effective use of brain potential through the encouragement of deliberate right-hemisphere function.

EEG CORRELATES OF ATTENTION IN HUMANS*

Frederick J. Bremner, V. Benignus, and F. Moritz, Trinity University, San Antonio, Texas

This study was supported by the Mind Science Foundation, Los Angeles, California. The authors express their appreciation to Mr. José Silva for his participation in the experiment and to David L. Carlson for his help in preparing the manuscript.

An attention model has been presented by Bremner and his co-workers which makes use of EEG changes as a dependent variable (Bremner, 1970; Ford, Morris, and Bremner, 1968; Eddy, Bremner, and Thomas, 1971; Hurwitz and Bremner, 1972). This model considers that there are different classes or subsets of attention but that, while these subsets are orthogonal, they are not arranged in a hierarchy. The subsets already defined are: expectancy, counter-expectancy, orientation, arousal, and non-focus (Hurwitz and Bremner, 1972).

The utility of the above model will increase as its generality increases. The present study attempts to extend the generality of the model from the animal data used for its original conception to data concerning human attentional states. The present study concentrated on two aspects of generalizing the model. One of these aspects was to see if human EEG was sensitive to changes relative to any of the

* "EEG Correlates of Attention in Humans" has since been published in *Neuropsychologia*, Vol. 10, 1972, pp. 307–12.

previously proposed subsets. The other aspect was to determine if there was any unique attentional subset present in humans but either not present in animals or not testable in animals.

Because much of the experimentation used to test the model has been directed toward the expectancy subset, this was the subset chosen to test human attention. The reader is reminded that expectancy is used here to mean that the subjects (Ss) have learned a relationship that stimulus B follows stimulus A.

Since the details of the procedure will be elaborated in the method section, suffice it to say that this will be done by means of a classical conditioning paradigm. This paradigm followed as closely as possible that used to gather the animal data. The animal data, however, capitalized on the ready availability of Theta rhythm. Human EEG data on the other hand are characterized by high probability of Alpha rhythm. Therefore Alpha rhythm was used as data for the dependent variable. The second aspect of this study may well be the more interesting. Psychologists have often debated the existence of a human inner consciousness. The present model addresses itself to this question by making internal focus a subset of attention. The internal-focus subset is characterized by the absence of exteroceptive stimulus and by being testable only in the human. It is proposed that this subset can be measured by EEG changes that occur following Ss responses during meditational and deep relaxation states.

METHOD

Subjects: The Ss were 20 volunteer male college students from an introductory psychology class, ranging in age from eighteen to twenty-five. They were told that the experiment was about self-control of brain waves, and were assigned irregularly to two groups of 10 Ss each.

Apparatus: A Beckman Type T electroencephalograph was used. Electrodes were stainless steel, attached subcutaneously over the vertex and occipital area. EEG data were visually monitored as well as tape recorded. Through an auditory biogenic feedback system, the brain waves in the Alpha range (8–13 Hz) could be filtered from the occipital EEG and presented to the S through earphones as an analog of the Alpha frequency. A Digital Equipment Corporation logic programmer was arranged to indicate a binary number, turn on a half-second CS, and 10 seconds later to turn on a 10-second UCS. The CS was a click delivered to the earphones worn by the subject, and consisted of the opening and closing of a relay connected to a six-volt battery. The UCS was a Grass PS 2 Photostimulator strobe light set at the S's eyes-closed Alpha frequency. All data were recorded on an 8-track Ampex Sp 300 Analog tape deck, and the completed analog tape was digitized by an A-D converter connected to an IBM 360/44 computer before analysis.

Procedure: This experiment was reviewed and approved by a University Committee for Humane Treatment of Humans as Experimental Subjects. Each S was asked to fill out a protocol sheet asking for such information as last use of alcohol or drugs, history of epileptic seizures, and previous experience with hypnosis, Yoga, or Alpha conditioning. In addition, the first time a S was brought into the lab, he was asked to sign a statement consenting to participate in the experiment and asserting that the nature and purpose of the procedure had been explained to him.

A baseline EEG was run on each S, with no feedback provided. The S was given a "close eyes" instruction as a stimulus. The graph was marked with a binary number, and separate recording channels were used for the unfiltered and filtered brain waves. This procedure was then repeated with an "open eyes" instruction. The S's face was monitored with closed-circuit television, and the total time in the chamber for the baseline data was approximately 30 minutes for each S. If the baseline reading was inadequate, the baseline procedure was repeated until artifact-free data were obtained.

Following the baseline procedure, Ss were divided into two groups of 10 Ss each. One group (Silva) was given a 14-hour weekend session of the José Silva Mind Control training course (Shah, 1971). While the Silva "mind control technique" is unique unto itself, it capitalizes on both deep relaxation and group hypnosis–like procedures. Some time is also spent in what best can be described as ESP exercises. At the beginning of the following week, the Ss were brought into the lab, and an EEG was taken for 20 minutes. Recordings were made both with eyes closed and with eyes open, while the Ss were practicing their Silva technique. On another occasion, an EEG was taken on the same Ss, with auditory biogenic feedback under similar instructions.

The second group (CC) of 10 Ss was run through a classical conditioning paradigm of 50 trials per session. Each trial consisted of a CS of a half-second click, followed by a 10-second interstimulus interval (ISI), followed by a UCS consisting of 10 seconds' duration of a strobe light set at the S's eyes-closed Alpha frequency. The intertrial interval (ITI) was irregular, with the experimenter starting the trial when S appeared relaxed. No feedback was provided for this set of trials. A 50-trial session lasted 20 to 30 minutes, and the sessions were repeated until S was conditioned to produce Alpha, or until the experimenter was convinced S could not produce Alpha sufficiently. The final 50-trial session was conducted for the CC group with biogenic feedback provided. All classical conditioning data reported were taken under eyes-open conditions.

TREATMENT OF RESULTS

For purposes of analysis, the EEG data were sampled in terms of epochs, one epoch being 10 consecutive seconds of data. For the baseline data, one epoch was taken for each S under eyes-closed and one epoch under eyes-open conditions. For the Silva Ss, after the 14-hour training session, one epoch was taken for eyes-closed, and one epoch for eyes-open conditions, without feedback. Eyes-closed and eyes-open epochs were also taken on the Silva group when feedback was provided. For the CC group, an early trial (trial 3 if it was artifact-free) was taken, and the epoch was the 10-second ISI. A similar epoch was taken from the last trial before the biogenic feedback, and a final epoch was taken after the feedback was started.

Each epoch was A-D converted and spectrally analyzed, yielding the power at various EEG frequencies (Walter, 1968). Only the eyes-open data will be reported in this paper.

RESULTS

Figures I and II (p. 229), summarize the results of the CC group and Silva group respectively. The effect of biogenic feedback can also be seen in each figure. The three aspects of the experiment were projected on a common axis; thus a comparison between baseline readings, improvement in Alpha frequency production through either experimental procedure, and the influence of biogenic feedback can be observed on the figure for each group.

Turning first to the CC group (Figure I), a definite increase in Alpha production due to the CC procedure is indicated by a peak in the middle line at frequencies 8 to 9 Hz. The baseline data did not appear to indicate a dominant Alpha rhythm output, as seen by the broad and rather flat spectra. The increase in mean percent power is distributed among a smaller number of frequencies. An additional change in the Alpha band is observed when biogenic feedback is introduced, and this is accompanied by a further narrowing of the spectra. That is, the introduction of biogenic feedback yielded yet another frequency shift.

Similar observations can be made of the Silva group data (Figure II) but caution must be exercised in comparing the figures of the two groups. Observation of the figure, however, indicates that the Silva Ss were quite capable of producing the Alpha rhythm following treatment, although not in the quantity demonstrated by the CC Ss. (See Figure I.) Again a downward frequency shift occurred and it appears to be greater here than in the CC group. This conclusion may not be entirely correct because the Silva group baseline readings included elevated production of higher frequencies, such as in the 10 to 12 Hz range, while baseline readings in the CC group did not. It is difficult, therefore, to make a judgment on the degree of relative shift in the two groups. It is worth noting, however, that the frequency shift occurred in the same direction in both groups and that the biogenic feedback had the same effect in both cases. (See Figure II.)

DISCUSSION

The data reported above would apparently support the Bremner attention model, particularly the expectancy and internal-focus subsets. It is rather interesting to compare the human data recorded in this study with animal data originally used to define the expectancy subset. (See Figure III.) If one compares Figures I and III, a certain similarity becomes apparent. The baseline and CS alone curves are broad and flat, while the conditioning curves are peaked. Also, both graphs show a frequency shift. The authors realize that the frequency shift is in the opposite direction. This is attributed to the fact that the animal data are from hippocampal sites while the human data are most closely associated with the occipital cortex. It seems, therefore, that expectancy as conceived by the model is correlated with the shape of the spectra and a frequency shift. Other authors have reported frequency shifts in human Alpha rhythm that would support an expectancy subset (Knott and Henry, 1941; Williams, 1940) or at least a correlation of Alpha with attention (Jasper and Shagass, 1940).

It is the contention of the authors that the subset internal focus is demonstrated by Figure II. These Ss trained in the Silva Mind Control system used no external stimuli to generate their data but rather what can best be described as mental imagery. One of the values of the Bremner model in this regard is that by defining the subset "internal focus" it becomes unnecessary to use terms such as "consciousness" or "mental imagery." Internal focus depends on antecedent conditions, such as instructions to the Ss, and on the EEG changes observed. It is of course realized that additional controls will be needed in order to test the reliability and validity of the internal-focus subset. This is particularly true in the light of Harts's (1968) criticism that Ss left to themselves in a dimly lit, quiet room for several minutes will increase their Alpha production. The present study (and Brown, 1970) may not be as vulnerable to this criticism, since it makes use of frequency shifts and shape of spectrum as opposed to those studies which rely on quantity or amplitude of Alpha (Kamiya, 1968). Nevertheless, it is interesting to speculate about the additional frequency shift following introduction of the biogenic feedback. In the case of the CC group it might have served to make the UCR and CR more overt, thus changing the classical conditioning paradigm into an instrumental conditioning situation with a CR of high incentive value. For the Silva-trained group, on the other hand, the feedback might make explicit to the Ss a correlate of internal focus that is not subjective.

INTERNAL FOCUS AS A SUBSET OF ATTENTION

Frederick J. Bremner and F. Moritz,
Trinity University, San Antonio, Texas

This study was supported by the Mind Science Foundation, Los Angeles, California, and the authors express their appreciation to Mr. José Silva for his participation in the experiment.

ABSTRACT

This report attempts to marshal more evidence on internal focus of attention in humans. The theoretical model used capitalizes on changes in EEG states as the dependent variable and a verbal command of the experimenter to start Alpha generation as the independent variable, in order to predict internal focus of attention.

In a previous publication (Bremner, et al., 1972) it was suggested that internal focus was a subset of attention and this subset was definable by certain antecedent conditions and certain characteristic EEG changes. The EEG changes were the generation of Alpha rhythm triggered by stimuli used as independent variables. This previous study was vulnerable to criticism, since Hart had reported (1968) that some Ss left to themselves in a dimly lit quiet room for several minutes will increase their Alpha production. It was reasoned, however, that if S could start and stop the generation of Alpha frequencies simultaneously with some signal from the experimenter this would satisfy the question of spurious appearance of Alpha frequencies as reported by Hart. If in addition this initiation of Alpha rhythm was related to S's verbal report of being internally focused it would provide collateral evidence in support of an internal-focus subset.

METHOD

Subjects: Ten men and women previously trained to generate Alpha rhythm served as subjects. Some of these were those used in the earlier experiment (Bremner, et al., 1972); nevertheless, all of the Ss reported having considerable experience in generating Alpha and conditioned deep relaxation as well as having had some experience with psychic exercises.

Apparatus: A Beckman type T electroencephalograph was used. Electrodes were stainless steel, attached subcutaneously over the vertex and occipital areas. EEG data were visually monitored as well as tape recorded. Additionally, a microphone hooked into the tape deck was supplied to the S so that his verbal account of his experience could be tape recorded. A Digital Equipment Corporation logic programmer was arranged to indicate a binary number on the record. The S's face and upper torso were monitored with a closed-circuit television camera. All data were recorded on an 8-track Ampex Sp 300 Analog tape deck.

Procedure: Each S filled out a protocol sheet asking for such information as last use of alcohol or drugs, history of epileptic seizures, and previous experience with hypnosis or deep-relaxation techniques. In addition, each S was required to sign a statement consenting to participate in the experiment and asserting that the nature and purpose of the procedure had been explained to him. Each S was told to generate Alpha by whatever method he was accustomed to using. A baseline run lasting approximately 5 minutes was made with S's eyes closed. Ten minutes more or less were spent in what can be best described as ESP exercises (Silva Method; McKnight, 1972) in order for the S to establish a point of reference for Alpha generation. The Ss were then asked to generate Alpha upon verbal command of the experimenter while their eyes were closed. When in the opinion of the experimenter enough EEG data indicated S was indeed generating Alpha, approximately 30 seconds later S was given the command to "stop Alpha." The start-stop command was given until the experimenter felt S was adequately demonstrating his ability and the record was sufficiently artifact free. The S was then given the instruction to "open eyes" and the same start-stop procedure was continued. None of the Ss in this study evidenced difficulty generating Alpha; however, some could not always cease Alpha production upon command, especially when their eyes were closed. Total time in the chamber for the entire procedure was approximately 45 minutes.

RESULTS

The results of the study are presented in Figures IV and V. Although the study was originally designed so that the data could be spectrally analyzed, the contrast between Alpha and non-Alpha was so well defined the experimenters felt that statistical analysis was unnecessary. Figure IV contains the data for 4 Ss with their eyes closed. The S symbol on the record (see Figure IV) indicates the start command while the T (terminate) indicates the command to stop. Note the contrast between the saw-toothed structure of the Alpha and the decreased amplitude of the record following the command to terminate. Figure V contains data for a set of 5 Ss, 3 Ss with eyes closed and 2 Ss—P8 and T9—with their eyes open (see Figure V). It is interesting to note that S T9 with his eyes open has a several-second lag after the start command before beginning to generate Alpha rhythm. This was consistent in all trials with this S with eyes open. It was demonstrated by S 5 with eyes closed, and was fairly characteristic of this S. It was also occasionally demonstrated by some of the other Ss.

The verbal report of all of the above Ss was that they were in a particular recognizable attentional state. All but one of the above Ss were able to predict when they were generating Alpha and when they were not. In other words, the Ss could say "start" and "stop" and the record would look the same as Figures IV and V.

DISCUSSION

The results given above would indicate that at least for this group of Ss the generation of Alpha rhythm is not spurious. Thus this group of Ss is less vulnerable to the kind of error pointed out by Hart (1968).

The lag time for some Ss is very interesting, but the authors can find no ready explanation of why recruiting takes so long in these Ss. Nevertheless, there was a relationship between the onset of Alpha rhythm in the EEG, the subject's unique subjective feeling, and the subject's verbal response that he was at a particular state of attention we choose to call the internal-focus subset.

REFERENCES

Bremner, F. J. "The effect of habituation and conditioning trials on hippocampal EEG." *Psychonomic Science*, 1970, 18, 181–83.

Brown, B. B. "Recognition of aspects of consciousness through association with alpha activity represented by a light signal." *Psychophysiology*, 1970, 6, 442–52.

Eddy, D. R., F. J. Bremner, and A. A. Thomas. "Identification of the precursors of hippocampal theta rhythm—a replication and extension." *Neuropsychologia*, 1971, 9, 43–50.

Ford, J. G., M. D. Morris, and F. J. Bremner. "The effect of drive on attention." *Psychonomic Science* 1968, 11, 156–57.

Hart J. T. "Autocontrol of EEG alpha." *Psychophysiology*, 1968, 4, 506. (Abstract.)

Hurwitz, S. L., and F. J. Bremner. "Hippocampal correlates of a conditioned sniffing response." *Neuropsychologia*, 1972.

Jasper, H. D., and C. Shagass. "Conditioning the occipital alpha rhythm in man." *Journal of Experimental Psychology*, 1941, 28 (5), 373–87.

Kamiya, J. "Conscious control of brain waves." *Psychology Today*, 1968, 1 (April), 57–60.

Knott, J., and C. Henry. "The conditioning of the blocking of alpha rhythm of the human electroencephalogram." *Journal of Experimental Psychology*, 1941, 28, 134–44.

McKnight, H. *Silva Mind Control Through Psychorientology*. Laredo, Tx.: Institute of Psychorientology, Inc., 1972.

Shah, D. "The alpha state lets the mind take wings." *The National Observer*, 1971, 34, 1, 16.

Walter, D. O. "Spectral analysis for electroencephalogram: mathematical determination of neurophysiological relationship from records of limited duration." *Experimental Neurology*, 1963, 8, 155–81.

Williams, A. C. "Facilitation of the alpha rhythm of the electroencephalogram." *Journal of Experimental Psychology*, 1940, 26, 413–22.

EEG CORRELATES OF ATTENTION
IN HUMANS

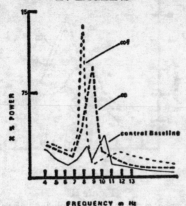

Figure I

Power spectra for the classical conditioning group, showing baseline (control), conditioning (CC), and biogenic feedback (CC-f) data.

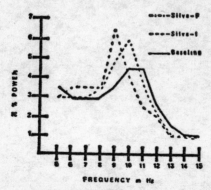

Figure II

Power spectra for Silva-trained group, showing baseline data, training data (Silva 1), and biogenic feedback data (Silva-f).

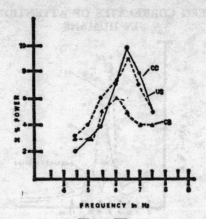

Figure III
Power spectra for hippocampal data of rats during classical conditioning (CC) and habituation of a light (CS).

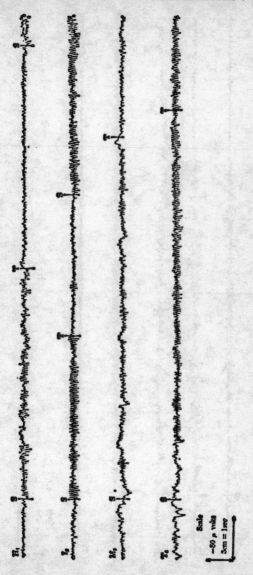

Scale
−50 μ volts
3cm = 1sec

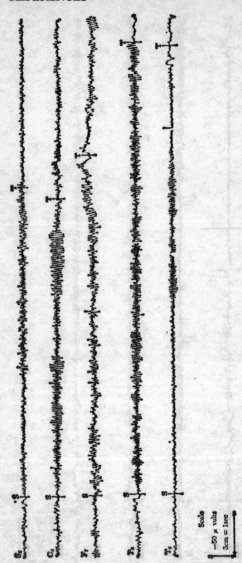

INDEX

$ FIND A BETTER JOB!

IMPROVE YOUR PRESENT ONE!

SECURE YOUR FINANCIAL FUTURE!

Get the guidance and the understanding you need in these top-selling books of advice, analysis and how-to-do-it expertise!

____ 42678 **CRISIS INVESTING**
by Douglas R. Casey $3.50

____ 47038 **COMPLETE RESUME BOOK AND JOB-GETTERS GUIDE**
by Dr. Juvenal Angel $3.95

____ 62203 **COMPLETE REAL ESTATE ADVISOR**
by Daniel J. deBenedictis $4.50

____ 49890 **MANAGERIAL WOMAN**
by Margaret Hennig and Anne Jardim $3.95

____ 62204 **SALESWOMAN: A Guide to Career Success**
by Barbara A. Pletcher $3.95

____ 61963 **MONEY TALKS**
by Robert W. Kent, editor (trade size) $7.95

____ 61914 **STRATEGIC INVESTING**
by Douglas Casey $4.95

USE THE COUPON BELOW TO ORDER

POCKET BOOKS, Department FAB
1230 Avenue of the Americas,
New York, N.Y. 10020

Please send me the books I have checked above. I am enclosing $_____ (please add 75¢ to cover postage and handling for each order. N.Y.S. and N.Y.C. residents please add appropriate sales tax). Send check or money order—no cash or C.O.D.'s please. Allow up to six weeks for delivery. For purchases over $10.00, you may use VISA: card number, expiration date and customer signature must be included.

NAME _____

ADDRESS _____

CITY _____ STATE/ZIP _____

934